CORPUS PALLADIANUM

VOLUME IV

CENTRO INTERNAZIONALE DI STUDI DI ARCHITETTURA
« ANDREA PALLADIO »

BOARD OF ADVISORS

CORPUS PALLADIANUM

Editor of the Series: Renato Cevese

Assistant Editor: Abelardo Cappelletti

THE LOGGIA

Arnaldo Venditti

THE LOGGIA
DEL CAPITANIATO

With a note on the pictorial decoration
by Franco Barbieri

THE PENNSYLVANIA STATE UNIVERSITY PRESS
UNIVERSITY PARK & LONDON

GILDA D'AGARO, in collaboration with Maria Tarlà and Mario Tomasutti, executed the scale drawings of the Basilica, the Redentore, and the Rotonda and, with the collaboration of Pietro Pelzel, those of the Malcontenta and the Convento della Carità. Andrzej Pereswiet-Sołtan, under the direction of Mario Zocconi, executed the drawings for the Villa Badoera, the Loggia Bernarda, the Palazzo Barbaran Da Porto, the Palazzo Da Porto Festa, the Villa Godi Malinverni, the Villa Pisani at Bagnolo, the Villa Pisani at Montagnana, the Villa Pojana, and the Teatro Olimpico. Mario Zocconi provided those of the Palazzo Antonini and the Villa Emo, the latter in collaboration with Andrzej Pereswiet-Sołtan.

The preparation of the monographs of the Corpus Palladianum has been made possible with the aid of the Consiglio Nazionale delle Ricerche of Italy and of the Enti Fondatori of the Centro Internazionale di Studi di Architettura "Andrea Palladio" in Vicenza.

I owe a debt of gratitude to the Centro Internazionale di Studi di Architettura " Andrea Palladio" for having given me the opportunity to carry out these studies. I am particularly grateful to Rodolfo Pallucchini, Roberto Pane, and Rudolf Wittkower for the invaluable contributions they have made to the progress of my research, with their ideas and criticism, and to Renato Cevese for his unfailing and generous assistance. I would also like to thank Mario Zocconi and Andrzej Pereswiet-Sołtan for the accurate scale drawings illustrating this essay, and the Comune and the Aziende Industriali Municipalizzate of Vicenza, who made the execution of these scale drawings possible.

A. V.

CONTENTS

THE LOGGIA DEL CAPITANIATO

a) - Loggia del Capitaniato: general view

HISTORY OF THE BUILDING

STRUCTURES ANTEDATING PALLADIO'S LOGGIA

The first seat of the Veronese " Capitaniato " during the second half of the fourteenth century—after Vicenza had fallen under the sway of the Scaligeri in 1314—appears to have been the palace of the patrician Verlato family, confiscated as the result of a plot in which its members had been involved.[1] At the end of the century a public loggia was erected in front of this palace, facing onto the main square of the city.[2] Other buildings in the square included the " Palatium vetus " and the " Palatium Communis,"[3] on the site now occupied by the Basilica (or Palazzo della Ragione)[4] and the high Torre dei Bissari, municipal property since 1226.[5]

In 1409, subsequent to the erection of the " lodia " or " lodia magna " and four years after the city had agreed of its own free will to submit to the Serenissima, the piazza was redesigned. No precise visual evidence[6] or descriptions relating to the building or the area in which it stood have survived. We may suppose, however, that the general layout which was later adopted by Palladio in his work of renovation must already have existed. There was a ground-floor portico used as a meeting-place and for the discussion of business affairs, with a corresponding reception hall on the upper floor for the captain; a balcony from which the populace could be addressed gave onto the square, according to the medieval scheme which Fra Giocondo in Verona had been the first to elaborate during the second half of the Quattrocento.[7]

Documents record the damage done to the building by the troops of the League of Cambrai in 1509, through political antipathy, since it symbolized the dominion of Venice. They also record the subsequent restoration carried out under the direction of the Venetian captain Alvise Foscari between 1520 and 1521, a restoration which also involved the site on which Palazzo Verlato stood, together with the remnants of various medieval structures. Among the names of artists employed on the building, those of the Vicentine painters Silvestro and Girolamo Dal Toso and Francesco Petolono are mentioned in connection with the decoration of the upper hall. The architect Giovanni da Porlezza, called " da Pedemuro," to whom the youthful Palladio was apprenticed,[8] is recorded as having carved the door leading from the hall to the captain's chancellery, " cum sancto Marco et figuris circum circa ";[9] the same master is mentioned in 1521, together with Antonio Abbondi (" lo Scarpagnino "), as having laid out the floor of the Loggia in white and red stone.[10]

During this restoration the coats-of-arms of Alvise Foscari and Tommaso Moro were placed on the façade of the Loggia, and in 1524 Titian's brother Francesco Vecellio was summoned with Paris Bordone to decorate the upper hall.[11] Guglielmo da Bergamo is recorded as having carved the wooden seats and the gates closing off the entrance to the Loggia. The latter works were completed by 1521. Twenty years later Giovanni da Pedemuro and his associate, Girolamo Pittoni, reappear, involved in the job of substituting a stone staircase for the ancient wooden one.[12] These works and others of less importance carried out between 1531 and 1538[13] seem to have been executed with some negligence, since less than half a century later it was rumored that the Loggia was on the verge of collapsing. Apart from its ruinous condition,[14] the building was at this time considered to be totally inadequate in size to accommodate the continually expanding public business.

THE CONSTRUCTION OF PALLADIO'S BUILDING

The first proposal to replace the building with a larger one was raised on 31 January 1565, when it was suggested that the houses adjacent to the Loggia up to the corner of the Contra' dei Giudei (the present-day Via Cavour) should be purchased and demolished to make room for the new structure (Fig. XIV).[15] This project was never carried out. An examination of the minutes of the municipal council during this period shows that collecting funds went very slowly.[16] Small sums were allotted every few months: in April of 1571 the sum of 300 ducats was voted and entrusted to two influential citizens, Giulia-

no Piovene and Giulio Bonifacio, who as " presidenti " of the building commission were to be held responsible for the proper administration of the funds.[17] A shrewd critic has pointed out that the document concerning the payment of this first sum mentions the proposal that the Loggia should be entirely refashioned (the phrase used is " ad refficionem lodiae ") rather than restored in its existing form; it is therefore legitimate to suppose that a certain number of experts had already been consulted, among them Palladio, whose presence in the city since February of the same year is attested.[18]

The sum having soon proved to be inadequate for the financing of any further work, the council met during the month of August 1571 and allocated another 300 ducats for the project. Only two months later, on October 25th, a third request for money shows (as Magrini has pointed out)[19] how cautiously the councilors were proceeding, and with what psychological subtlety, in their demands for such small sums, for by so doing they did not incur the risk of refusal that they might have encountered by requesting a larger one.

Satisfactory progress on the work of restoration was reported in October 1571, and the hope was expressed that it might be finished by St. Martin's Day. In November the council was requested to grant the sum necessary to complete the roof covering the restored section,[20] and on December 23rd a final allocation was approved by an almost unanimous vote.[21] A mere three days[22] later the " signori deputati " conceded another small sum but declared that further funds would not be available.[23] The sums granted during the month of November must have been intended for work connected with the construction of the side of the building, for this is in the form of a triumphal arch and must have been erected after the victory of the bat-

I - MARCO MORO, *Piazza dei Signori seen from the west.* From *Vicenza e i suoi dintorni*, 1850

tle of Lepanto on October 7th of that year, news of which had reached Vicenza on October 18th.[24]

The principal façade of the Loggia was embellished with the name of the Venetian captain in office that year, Giambattista Bernardo (JO. BAPTISTAE BERNARDO PRAEFECTO; Plate 9), and with an inscription rendering homage and thanks to him for the work he had done in the interests of the city. This recognition was fully merited; it was due not to the flattery customary during the period, as Magrini would have it,[25] but to the fact that Bernardo bore the greater part of the expense of reconstruction in person,[26] notwithstanding the contributions granted by the city fathers (these were paid as advances on incoming revenues from two sources: legal fines and the costs of citizenship paid by

new applicants for that honor). Various statues with inscriptions were placed along the side façade,[27] among them *Peace* and *Victory* in the two intercolumniations flanking the arch (Plates 32-33). These, together with the wealth of stucco bas-reliefs representing trophies (Plates 28-29), evidently commemorated the abovementioned victory.

The construction of the Loggia was then arrested at this stage, and it still exists in the same form (Plate 2)—which, as we shall see, represents only a part of the initial program. As soon as building operations stopped, the Vicentine artist Giovanni Antonio Fasolo, one of Paolo Veronese's pupils, was commissioned to paint nine canvases for the fields within the beamed ceiling covering the upper hall (Plates 50-51); by depicting famous events in Roman history, these were to serve as an exaltation of military virtues.[28] Since the painter died on 1 September 1572, we may consider that date to be a *terminus ante quem* for the completion of the Loggia[29] (under the reduced program), a fact that is further confirmed by the absence of other documents recording masonry work after that year. The Loggia must have been fulfilling its functions only a decade later, for in 1582 there is mention of work on the interior furnishings and of the removal of rubble still lying under the arches of the arcade.[30] Possibly the sum of 210 ducats paid at this time to a certain Battista di Guglielmo concerns these jobs.[31]

Thus the Loggia—which during the course of the Seicento was to be further embellished with paintings by Alessandro Maganza (1614), Francesco Maffei, and Giulio Carpioni (1656, 1665)[32]—was constructed in a very short space of time: actually during a few months in 1571, between April and December, with the interior being completed the following year.

PROBLEMS OF ATTRIBUTION
AND ALTERATIONS:
RESTORATION OR RECONSTRUCTION?

An analysis of the documents examined so far is not only insufficient to establish with any certainty the course of the building's construction, the chronological limits of which can be only approximately defined, but also presents two problems. The first of these concerns the attribution. No reference is made to Palladio, but the question can be resolved by a critical analysis of the building itself—every aspect of which reveals the master's hand, from the general impression to the minutest detail—and also by the inscription carved beneath the side balcony, which reads: " ANDREA

PALLADIO I[NVENTORE] ARCHIT." (Plates 19-20, 23).[33]

The absence of Palladio's name in the documents seems even more inexplicable when we consider that the structure in question is one of his last works, designed when his reputation was firmly established not only in Vicenza but also in Venice. Actually, the architect's transfer with his family to Venice, after he had been appointed architect to the Serenissima on Sansovino's death, and his sojourn there while he was involved in work on San Giorgio Maggiore were what prevented him from supervising building operations in Vicenza. We know that in March 1572, yielding to the insistence of several of the Vicentine councilors, he delivered to the permanent nuncio in Venice, Giovanni Battista Pigafetta, a number of " sagome... per dar al clarissimo Capitanio." These were devised to resolve some of the problems that had arisen during the erection of the Loggia. Palladio was unable to keep his promise to travel to Vicenza in order to resolve the questions the councilors had laid before him, because only two-and-a-half months after he had lost his eldest son, Leonida (who died in January of 1572), he was further stricken by the death of his son Orazio.[34]

In any case, the attribution of the design to Palladio is acknowledged today by all architectural historians and has never been questioned; on the contrary, it was already confirmed by local literature in the seventeenth century: Castellini's manuscript of 1628, describing the monuments of Vicenza, mentions Palladio as architect of the Loggia. More than a century was to pass before the first measured drawings of the building were done: Francesco Muttoni provided the rather coarse designs (Fig. IV) about the middle of the eighteenth century, on the commission of an Englishman[35]—which demonstrates the lively interest taken in London in Palladio's work after the publication of the *Quattro Libri* in Giacomo Leoni's edition of 1715[36] (and, even more important, after the publicity given to Palladio's designs by Lord Burlington through the publication of the architect's reconstructions of Roman baths, discovered at Maser among others of the architect's autograph drawings and now the property of the R.I.B.A. in London[37]).

The second problem posed by the documents concerns the extent of the work carried out in the Cinquecento. The documents do not make it clear whether the renovation of the Loggia was complete or only partial, i.e., whether the old Loggia was to be rebuilt "ex novo" after its demolition or whether it was only to be drastically restored. The building's coherent and unified form as it appears today (Plates 3-7) seems, notwithstanding Pée's opinion,[38] to justify the first hypothesis: that the ancient structure, condemned as on the verge of collapse in January 1565, underwent a process of total renovation. The fact that the adjacent sites up to the Contra' dei Giudei were never purchased cannot be adduced as proof in support of the alternative hypothesis that the restoration was merely partial, as has been suggested;[39] if anything, this would have compromised the full execution of the scheme initially decided upon. But neither does it permit us to conclude that the preexisting structures were reemployed. Moreover, Palladio's concept of "restoration" was not that of mere renovation in an historical sense, but of complete rebuilding, as other examples of his work clearly demonstrate. Examples are the Basilica, where he demolished the surviving loggias in order to refashion them according to his own formal principles; or his first designs for San Petronio, before he accepted a compromise between his own conception and the despised Gothic taste; or, finally, the typical case of the Doge's Palace in Venice, where he did not hesitate when called upon for advice after the fire of 1577 to propose a complete transformation of the building—which has fortunately survived intact, thanks to the more prudent restoration suggested by Antonio da Ponte.[40]

PALLADIO'S DESIGN

FORMAL ANALYSIS

The Loggia del Capitaniato today consists of a lower arcade and an upper storey (Scale Drawings *d, e*), both of which abut on the ancient Torre Verlata (Plates 18-19), with the Palladian building forming a kind of prolongation of the latter toward the piazza (before the extensive alterations effected by Vincenzo Scamozzi in 1592 for Count Galeazzo Trissino and the successive modifications wrought by Pizzocaro and Calderari).[41]

The earliest thorough analysis of the Loggia was made by Bertotti Scamozzi during the last two decades of the eighteenth century.[42] His point of departure was the feature characterizing the façade which gives onto the piazza (Plates 2-7), i.e., the giant order which Palladio had already used in Palazzo Valmarana and which was suggested by Michelangelo's designs for the Capitol: "L'ornamento del prospetto principale è formato da un ordine composito, le colonne del quale hanno tanta altezza che, con la loro trabeazione e l'attico che vi è sovrapposto, comprendono l'elevazione della loggia terrena e della sala superiore" (Scale Drawings *b, g*). The description continues: "Si entra per gli intercolumni nel piano terreno, sotto maestosi archi, sopra i quali sono aperte nel piano superiore delle finestre con poggiuoli, che sporgendo sono sostenute da robuste mensole o modiglioni. Portano le suddette colonne una proporzionata trabeazione, sopra cui v'è l'attico con pilastrini, tramezzo a' quali sonovi delle finestre che rendono dall'alto più luminosa la sala. Sopra la cornice cammina una balaustra tramezzata da piedistalli, che

stanno a piombo delle colonne, la quale compie vagamente il prospetto" (Plate 9).

The giant order, with its entablature and the balustrade topping the shafts of the columns (Plates 8-9, 16), is crowned by a pseudo-attic erected for the express purpose of illuminating the hall by a double row of apertures. Although this attic is clearly visible from the Basilica or the Piazza, it gradually recedes from view as one approaches the building and is quite indiscernible in a foreshortened view (Plates 14-15, 17), as it is blocked by the projecting members of the entablature. This solution is typical of the Loggia and may be found in a different and even more exaggerated form elsewhere: for example, at Palazzo Porto Breganze in Piazza Castello, where the attic as such is suppressed and is swallowed up by the sharply projecting entablature.

The absence of a straight entablature and of an attic directly connected with the architectonic members below it characterizes the Loggia in its own special fashion and confirms the impression that here Palladio was seeking a new formal solution. The transition between the attic and the structure beneath is effected by means of the balustrade (Plates 5, 11), which takes on an entirely new significance, far removed from the serenity with which the same morphological element had been used in the Basilica.

The smooth shafts of the columns form a strong contrast to the deep shadows under the three arches spanning the ground floor (Plate 10) and to the supports of the balconies of the main hall, whose balustrades rest on angular parallelepiped triglyphs. The latter appear, in their pre-

II - CRISTOFORO DALL'ACQUA, *Piazza dei Signori and Piazzetta Palladio*. From *Vedute vicentine*, 1770-80

cise reference to the formal vocabulary of Michelangelo, to be not only perfectly consonant with the interruption of the architrave by the balconies (Plates 12-13) but also to be totally unconnected with the lower order, "as if they were archaeological remains introduced by force into a new and different rhythm." [43] Having lost over the centuries the thin layer of plaster that formerly covered the columns,[44] giving them the sheen of white marble, the façade facing the Piazza now has a certain chromatic quality due to the uncovered brick surfaces of the columns and those around the windows: the stuccoes, modeled to represent military trophies celebrating the battle of Lepanto, have partially disappeared (Plates 11-13). This chromaticism is alien to Palladio's way of thinking, as he aimed at creating an "heroic and epic" impression in his later works, which was achieved by the use of monochromatic elements of varying projec-

tions, "as if to make use of the entire scale of chiaroscuro values, from the pitch-black of the entablature and the arches to the pearl-white of the shafts of the columns, while the smooth reliefs of the trophies have a subdued tone somewhat like the cloudy sky in one of Piranesi's etchings," as Pane has pointed out.[45] Here, too, white has no mimetic value; it is not used in imitation of marble but is ideally neutral and is eminently suited to Palladio's sense of plastic values.

The front façade gives a foretaste of the architect's aims as he was to carry them out with absolute coherence on the side one (Plate 4). The extraordinary originality of the composition—which is related only in an ideal sense to examples of Hellenistic architecture such as the Arch of Septimius Severus or the triumphal arch in Orange (to which one might say Palladio felt himself attracted through a "subconscious" sort

of affinity [46])—goes hand-in-hand with an
open and independent violation of the canons. This is evident not only in the proportions of the composite giant order, calculated (as Bertotti pointed out) according to
the measurements Palladio had himself
established for the Corinthian order,[47] but
also in the abrupt break in the architrave
of the giant order introduced by the frames
surrounding the rectangular window openings (Plates 9-13; Figures VIII, XI). This
bold solution, although consonant with the
feeling which Palladio intended to evoke
in the front façade as well as in the side
one, was criticized by Bertotti Scamozzi,
who failed to realize its significance and
judged it to be a " colossal flaw," due to
" arbitrary and not very accurate execution "
and not Palladio's own fault.[48] We might
add, in confutation of the thesis that Palladio was influenced by Mannerism, that
this solution is not only alien to the vertical
emphasis of the ashlar blocks forming the
architraves so familiar in buildings designed
by mannerist architects, but it is equally
void of intellectual pretense and of the
hedonistic virtuosity typical of Mannerism.

In designing the side façade, Palladio
kept in mind that the formal elements
would be less visible, since the side of the
Loggia faces onto a narrow street (Via del
Monte di Pietà), and adjusted his proportions accordingly (Plates 3-5, 20; Scale
Drawing *i*); this offers further testimony
of Palladio's gift for town-planning, as he
was ready to accept new suggestions due
to urban configuration or to natural condi-
tions (Fig. XV).[49] In this case, he rejected
the giant order and adopted an arrangement with a lower order of coupled columns flanking an arch almost identical to
those on the façade; the arch constitutes
the transitional element between the exterior and the interior space beneath the
portico, whose vault with its lunettes rests
on half-columns of equal height. The hall

above is lighted by an arched window of
smaller dimensions, flanked by two niches
framed at the top by short entablatures,
creating the impression of a Serliana, a
motif used by Palladio even in his earliest
buildings (Plate 22; Figs. IX, XII).[50]

STUCCOES AND SCULPTURAL
DECORATION: ICONOGRAPHY AND
INSCRIPTIONS

In discussing the iconography of the
stuccoes on the Loggia, we should remember
that only a portion of the military trophies
flanking the windows of the main façade
have survived (those on both sides of the
window at the left and the one on the
right side of the window at the right);
otherwise only traces of them remain on
the brickwork (Plates 11-13). The stuccoes
on the spandrels of the arches, enclosed
between the half-columns and the triglyphs,
represent nude, frowning, bearded river
gods pouring water from vases resting on
their shoulders (or, in the case of the
ones at the ends, almost on their bellies;
Plate 10). This arrangement, which is symmetrical if the three bays are considered
as a whole, reveals that at the time the
stuccoes were executed the idea of extending the building any further had already
been abandoned. A compromise dictated
by economic necessity transformed the
central bay into the definitive center of the
building; this is further confirmed not only
by the inscription on the frieze running
along the entablature but also by the decoration appearing between the triglyphs,
which is replaced beneath the central balcony by a slab commemorating the building, the city, and the captain: " SI QUAE
CELICOLAE MAGNI, VICENTIA PONIT — VOS
ARAE, ET CUM ARIS AUREA TEMPLA JU-
VANT; — INGENTUM HANC MOLEM AETER-
NUM SERVATE PER AEVUM, — PROTEGITE

III - ANDREA PALLADIO, *Project for a municipal loggia with five arcades of a composite order.*
Museo Civico, Vicenza, D. 19 r.

ET SECLIS INNUMERABILIBUS, — NAM-
QUE IPSAM AETERNO BERNARDI EREXIT
HONORI — GRATI AETERNA ANIMI SIGNA
FUTURA SUI." [51] On the other hand, between the triglyphs supporting the end
balconies we find cartouches with double
swags, which emphasize the curve of the
arch but do not detract from its geometric
development (Plates 12, 14-15).

The desire to stress the horizontal lines
of the façade in order to emphasize the
intersection of the orders, as in the Venetian churches, is evident not only in
the construction of the balustrade above
the cornice and in the attic storey, but also
in the manner in which the balconies are
joined to the wall behind: they are carried
above two short lengths of horizontal cornices which abut onto the half-columns
(Plate 10). By this contrivance Palladio was
able to place small bases adorned with

cartouches containing masks beneath the
military trophies flanking the windows, like
the bas-reliefs between the coupled columns
in the Chiesa del Redentore. The sharply
accentuated projection of the dentillated
upper cornice of the entablature (Scale
Drawings *h, j*) jutting out over the shafts
of the columns throws such a deep shadow
that it not only renders the inscription in
Augustan characters celebrating the captain
("JO. BAPTISTAE BERNARDO PRAEFECTO
CIVITAS DICAVIT") illegible at a distance,
but also tends to attenuate the dominant
horizontal line indicated above (Plates
2-4, 6).

The more lavish decoration along the
side shows two Victories in the spandrels
of the lower arch (Plates 20, 22-23), and
Palladio placed the curly head of a youth
crowned by a volute as the keystone upon
which the signed architrave rests (" AN-

DREA PALLADIO I. ARCHIT. "; Plate 23). The pairs of columns intersect the horizontal impost cornice, which corresponds to that of the arches along the façade; below this clearly defined line Palladio placed nothing but the statues on their pedestals, thus avoiding an overly exaggerated chiaroscuro effect which might have disturbed the classical serenity he intended. These statues, unlike the ones above which form part of the mannerist decoration behind them, seem to be a sort of typically Renaissance classical reference, echoed in the statues above set into the niches and in the Latin inscription. The statues seem to invite those who pass by to pause and exult in the victory. The female figure on the right, draped in a long tunic and shown in a contrapposto pose, stands on a base which has an inscription reading: " PALMAM GENUERE CARINAE "; she represents the goddess of naval victories (Plate 35). The female divinity on the left is wearing a cuirass but is shown in an attitude of repose, with her head resting on her left hand; the inscription " BELLI SECURA QUIESCO " confirms the fact that this is a personification of Peace after battle (Plate 34).[52]

Above the impost cornice of the lower arch and between the capitals of the columns are lavish swags over square-framed cartouches bearing heraldic symbols, one of the city (on the left), the other of the Bernardo family (Fig. IX; Plates 24-27). The swags repeat the motif of those in the niches of the Serliana (Plate 22) and are a motif which Palladio adopted from Sansovino's Tuscan style. The geometrical development is interrupted at each end by a delicate zone of chiaroscuro, in which three bands of fruit and flowers knotted with fluttering ribbons are set vertically below a mask to form a manneristic and extremely original sort of candelabrum. This is the style of the festoons flanking

the windows of the Palazzo Iseppo da Porto and the Palazzo Chiericati, with the addition of the dynamic motif of the ribbon, which vaguely recalls the splendid, continuous frieze running between the bucrania and paterae of the Convento della Carità.

Above the sharply accentuated horizontal line of the side façade, consisting of the cornice supporting the central balcony and recalling the balconies on the façade facing the piazza, we find the main display of stuccoes which adorns the Loggia. The two panels at the sides of the fluted pilasters flanking the Serliana are crowded with a series of stuccoes representing triumphal themes: a victor's cuirass is raised on a stake and flanked by a number of objects wrested from the vanquished, such as scimitars, axes, banners, helmets, and drums, in an elaborate but restrained scheme of ornamentation (Plates 28-29). The panels terminate in the abovementioned statues, which contribute a deep chiaroscuro to the extremities of the side, constituting—as in the Palazzo Valmarana—an intermediary member between Palladio's building and the surroundings; indeed, they provide on the left side a transitional motif between the major and minor orders characterizing the front and side façades (Plate 13; Scale Drawing i). The statue placed at the conjunction of the two façades shows a young warrior in a Roman helmet and cuirass holding a sling in his left hand and a stone in his right, while his foot rests on a tortoise. An inscription on the base of the statue reads: " UNI VIRTUTIS GENIO. " The statue either represents David, slayer of Goliath and symbol of heroism, or according to Wittkower, Virtus (Plate 28).[53] The corresponding statue on the right—a female figure with uncovered breasts in a long, close-fitting tunic, who has a cornucopia in her hand and a helmet under her foot—represents Honor (Plate 29), as the inscription on the base indicates: " DEA

NUBIT HONORIS." This phrase, together with the preceding one, forms a single hexameter signifying that " the goddess of Honor takes as her spouse none but the genius of Courage." This verse, like the others, is Renaissance and not antique.[54] At the beginning of the Seicento Ripa's *Iconologia* had already pointed out the connection between Honor and Virtue.[55]

The niches of the Serliana are occupied by two indifferent female statues, which are not easy to interpret; they seem to be allegories of civic virtues. One bears the inscription " DIIS THURE ET CORDE LI-BANDUM," the other the phrase " SORDES PIETAS UNA ABLUIT OMNES." The former, in the niche on the left, is draped in the classical manner and wears a cross on her breast; in her right hand she holds an amphora from which water gushes forth, and in her left one a censer, two objects which accompany the sacrifice offered up for victory (Plate 30). The figure on the right is a nude youth, holding on his arm a child (now headless) who carries an elephant head, with a stork at his side (Plate 31). The symbolic unity of the cycle —which we shall examine in detail later, with reference to contemporary literature— must have been explicated by the inscriptions in the cartouches placed below the stuccoed panels already described. Unfortunately the stone has crumbled away to such an extent that almost all the letters are indecipherable, and it is impossible to interpret them accurately. Wittkower favors the suggestion that the statues in the niches represent two Christian Virtues, *Fides* and *Pietas*, and thus he interprets the cycle as signifying that Virtue and Honor beneath the banners of Faith and Piety achieve Victory and Peace.

The pronounced chiaroscuro of the façade on Piazza dei Signori is repeated on the side, with the same river gods in the spandrels of the lower arch. These figures have more room to stretch out than those on the piazza façade do (Plates 22-23), because of the absence of modillions below the balconies; they also balance the lavish display of stuccoes in the broad, open spaces at the sides of the Serliana. Although, as we have already mentioned, the broad band of the dentillated entablature beneath the side balcony bears Palladio's name, once the architect had furnished the plan of the building and provided for the chiaroscuro effects of the construction as a whole, he entrusted the ornamental stuccoes to a sculptor whom Zorzi has identified as Lorenzo Rubini of Vicenza.[56] The latter is mentioned by Palladio in his *Quattro Libri* in connection with the statues on the podium arms flanking the stairs leading to the Rotonda;[57] he collaborated with Palladio on various occasions.[58] Lorenzo's career began in 1553 when he collaborated with Alessandro Vittoria in carving the caryatid on the right of the old entrance door to the Library of St. Mark's in Venice;[59] he may be considered one of Vittoria's followers, for he felt the latter's influence strongly, and in 1554 he married one of Vittoria's sisters.[60] An argument against the attribution of the Loggia stuccoes to his sons, Vigilio and Agostino,[61] derives from the fact that the stuccoes must have been begun in 1571, immediately upon the completion of the structure, and finished in 1575,[62] the year in which Lorenzo is presumed to have died. In 1571 Vigilio and Agostino were too young to be employed on a work of such scope, since one was only twelve years old and the other only eleven. The suggested attribution of the decorations to Ottaviano Ridolfi[63] does not appear to be justified either, for in 1572 he was still in Verona, arriving in Vicenza only in 1575. These chronological considerations are supported by a stylistic examination of the decorative cycle, which appears to be the work of a mature artist

IV - FRANCESCO MUTTONI, *Plan and elevations of the Loggia del Capitaniato.* From "Dissegni et Añotationi fatte di commissione del signor K.re Tuixden Inglese," MS in the Library of the C.I.S.A., n. 323

rather than of a beginner.[64] The main façade on Piazza dei Signori is adorned with the nude, bearded figures of river gods (Plates 9-16) imprisoned, as it were, between the giant shafts of the columns and the heavy balconies resting on triglyph-supports; these figures are among the more successful examples of mannerist sculpture in Vicenza and undoubtedly recall similar figures in the spandrels of the lower order of the Library of St. Mark's. The strong characterization and vigorous modeling, clear reminiscences of Michelangelo's style, are found again in the masks at the sides of the balconies, which serve as bases for the panels with military trophies flanking the windows, most of which have regrettably crumbled away.

The decoration on the side façade is crowded and restless. The bas-reliefs are accompanied by six statues with mottoes referring to the battle of Lepanto; the various representations of arms and military attributes, flanked by lavish festoons suspended from lions' heads similar to those in other buildings or designs, likewise refer to the same theme. Other masks and large cartouches embellished with imaginary constructions flank the sides of the central balcony (Plates 28-29). In Zorzi's opinion, the decoration of the upper zone of the façade is particularly confused and heavy, so much so that the architectural lines are destroyed, whereas the ornamentation of the lower zone (Plate 20) is far superior, because of the splendid winged Victories in the spandrels of the arches, the huge mask on the keystone, and the magnificent coats-of-arms of the city and of Captain Bernardo set below the festoons that link the capitals of the pairs of columns flanking the arches.[65] We must confess that we are not conscious of this incongruity between the two zones of the side façade, in which the chiaroscuro effects resulting from the interplay between openings and solid masses seem perfectly calculated both on the ground floor and on the upper storey; indeed, we might point out that the cavities of the niches flanking the upper arch beneath their architraves have the same chiaroscuro value that the columns below do, although they are concave rather than convex (Scale Drawing c); in fact, the integration between sculpture and architecture mediated in the lower zone through the high-relief effect of the half-columns is achieved above by means of the niches themselves (Plates 18-19), whose function in the composition would have been clearer if they had remained empty, for they would then have constituted a moment of repose amidst the pulsating pictorial effects surrounding them. In this way the two other statues in the upper zone, on bases corresponding to the shafts of the columns, would have assumed a very different visual significance, recalling those placed at the ends of the façade of Palazzo Valmarana, which function as terminal motifs.[66] Another element which induces one to imagine the niches of the upper Serliana as empty is represented by the pilasters, which, as in Casa Cogollo, are not smooth but are deeply scored with flutes.[67] Attention, however, should be chiefly drawn to the covered space of the portico, articulated with half-columns corresponding to the trabeation scheme which includes the imposts of the outer arches (Plates 39-40; Fig. XIII); this is a fortunate solution which constitutes a link between the pronounced chiaroscuro of the exterior and the sober linearity of the interior. By this means the cold, dim character of the Palazzo Thiene Bonin, resulting from the use of pilasters instead of columns on the side walls of the vestibule, has been avoided.[68]

As no documentary evidence exists, the question of attributing the statues on the side of the Loggia is still an open one. Several studies have been devoted to their allegorical meanings because their identities are not clear from the inscriptions. We are persuaded to conclude with Zorzi that those of Peace and Victory, representing personifications of Vicenza and Venice respectively (Plates 32-35), must be attributed to Lorenzo Rubini, and that the upper ones (the two in the niches mentioned above and those on the pedestals at the sides), seen from a greater distance, must have been left to his assistants. The details are much inferior in execution, and the works certainly do not reach Rubini's standards; nor do they reflect the elongated lines of figures produced by members of his school, influenced by a taste for the work of Parmigianino.[69]

In conclusion, we must point out that the archaizing tone of the decorative iconography of the Loggia is perfectly in accordance with Palladio's own poetic sensibility, which was rooted in that Renaissance spirit of which it has been said that he was the last representative. The present writer disagrees with Ackerman's implication that the content of the decoration was established independently of Palladio and that it involves an excess of sculpture which obscures the architectonic values of the construction.[70] On the contrary, we suggest that Palladio's intention was that architecture and decoration function inseparably, even if the actual execution of the latter was left to others. This appears to be fully demonstrated by comparing the organic synthesis of chiaroscuro values achieved between architectural and stucco elements throughout Palladio's work, from the Palazzo Porto Barbaran to Palazzo Angarano and the Loggia del Capitaniato.

THE RELATIONSHIP BETWEEN THE FRONT AND SIDE FAÇADES

The major critical problem posed by the Loggia is that of the relationship of the front façade to the side one, because of the singular change of rhythm employed by Palladio between these two sides, the only ones to have been erected (Plates 3-4). In commenting upon this peculiarity, Wittkower has suggested that Palladio must have been obliged to interrupt the uniform continuity of rhythm he had planned after the news of the battle of Lepanto, abandoning the scheme used on the front to provide a triumphal arch on the side of the Loggia (Scale Drawings b, c):[71] " It is surprising, and contrary to Palladio's normal practice, that the system of the main front is not carried on at the side ... Political actuality overruled considerations of artistic principle. It seems justified to conclude that Palladio sacrificed an originally uniform plan to the exigencies of the victory." [72] In other words, according to this interpretation the change of rhythm would not have been planned by Palladio but would have been imposed upon him by outward circumstances, thus giving rise to an utterly unacceptable compromise in which the organic quality of the whole structure was sacrificed, despite the juxtaposition of the two façades, which makes the discontinuity less evident. Not even the syntactic repetitions occurring in the two façades—the continuous level of the impost cornices bearing the arches, the cornices of the balconies, and the entablature at the crown (Plates 7, 17)—would suffice to justify such a striking difference in composition.

Wittkower's thesis is accepted by Ackerman, who suggests that changes in the project were hastily improvised after the news of the victorious battle of Lepanto had reached Vicenza. He proposes that the side façade (Plate 18) was transformed into a triumphal arch with statues of Peace and Victory on the lower storey and a field for trophies and allegories of civic virtues above; he concedes, however, that the trophies may also refer to the protective role of the captain.[73]

In rejecting Wittkower's hypothesis, Pane sought to establish the validity of the poetical image realized by Palladio in the absolute formal coherence of the structure, a coherence evident not only in the chiaroscuro effect which dominates the ensemble, but also in the fact that the unexpected change in rhythm is matched by an equally unusual articulation and proportion in all the elements.[74] On the other hand, he adds a purely logical objection to the hypothesis to this formal one: during the months in which the Loggia was being rapidly erected under the prefect Giovanni Battista Bernardo, the war against the Turks was also being waged; it is therefore logical to suppose that Palladio had already prepared a triumphal composition with conciliatory overtones. This is a much more likely possibility than the idea that he would have designed a project totally extraneous to such a stirring episode in Italian history, which at the time must have been of primary interest and concern to everyone. We might add, moreover, that re-employing the giant order on the side façade would have been inconsistent with Palladio's sensitivity to town-planning, for had he repeated the motif there it would have meant that he had forgotten to take into consideration the different relationship between the width of the street and the body of the building (Scale Drawing a).

Concerning the triumphal character of the whole building (Scale Drawing c), Wittkower is not content simply to observe that each decorative detail seems to allude to the great naval victory, but adds that " Palladio's building would thus appear to be a monumental symbol of victory like the

triumphal arches of antiquity." [75] In addition, according to an ingenious theory of Wittkower's, "... there existed for Palladio a deep affinity between the monumental loggia and the triumphal arch "; to demonstrate this, he cites the decoration Palladio designed for the official visit to Venice of Henry III of France, en route from Poland to Paris. This temporary structure of wood and stucco—the technique customarily used for the decorations and spectacles which were rapidly becoming a commonplace of Italian life at the turn of the Cinquecento—seems to have been a cross between a triumphal arch and a monumental loggia. Judging from Andrea Vicentino's painting in the Doge's Palace depicting the decoration (although we cannot tell how accurately),[76] a loggia of giant Corinthian columns rose behind the triumphal arch, the columns equal in height to those of the arch in front, " thereby manifesting that assembly and triumph are closely interrelated." [77] This statement seems over-generalized and is consequently subject to historical contradiction: it is sufficient to consider the nature of other structures planned for assemblies, such as the Loggia del Consiglio by Fra' Giocondo in Verona, or the sedili of southern Italian towns, such as the Sedile Dominova at Sorrento, those of Aversa and Lecce, or the since-destroyed ones in Naples. Wittkower's hypothesis is only partly acceptable, although it may seem valid in Palladio's case. The architect had insisted on the triumphal-arch theme as the major feature of the decoration he planned immediately on his return from Venice for the entrance into Vicenza of Bishop Priuli in 1565, which Magrini has described from documents in the archives; it was erected on the Ponte degli Angeli. The proscenium for the Teatro Olimpico, executed on Palladio's designs after his death,[78] also incorporates the scheme of the triumphal arch, enlivened by perspective views of

V - FRANCESCO MUTTONI, *Elevation and plan of the Loggia del Capitaniato with a hypothetical five-bay façade.*
From *Architettura di Andrea Palladio Vicentino...*, Venice, 1760, IX, pls. VII-X

streets which were intended to give a theatrical impression of an urban setting. Chastel also states that Palladio often seems intent on emphasizing the relationship between a triumphal arch (which was used during the Renaissance in modernized versions for city gates) and a loggia behind it, the former serving to solemnize the entrance into the city or building, the latter to ennoble the guest's reception; the "columnatio" was reserved for the urban scene as a symbol of the collective participation of the whole city in an historical occasion.[79] Quite possibly the arch and loggia, elements adopted by Palladio in a typical central-Italian manner when he prepared the decorations for Henry III's visit,[80] were applied to the Loggia del Capitaniato but were fused into a single structure in such a highly original way that it is impossible to classify the result, which represents the symbolic integration of the Basilica standing opposite, among any established types or models (Fig. I; Plates 20, 39).

THE INTERIOR

The interior of the Loggia del Capitaniato demonstrates Palladio's rare capacity to furnish an unending series of images through the interrelationships of walls and columns in the lower storey (i.e., the portico); in the upper storey (the hall), he obtains his effects by means of a skillful study of the interplay of proportions and of sources of light, while renouncing any decided articulation of the various architectonic members (Figs. VI, XIII).

The interior of the portico gains its appearance of unity through the series of vaults which have equal dimensions along both the front facing the Basilica (Plates 39, 45) and the side (Plates 40-41). The giant order of the exterior is not seen from the interior. On the exterior of the piazza

façade the piers which support the vault are faced by the imposing Corinthian half-columns, but on the interior face this effect is softened by using a series of smaller half-columns and corner pilasters, reduced to proportions suiting the interior dimensions and topped by an architrave and cornice (Scale Drawings d, f; Plates 42-43). The cornice is one of the more significant elements in this composition, as it forms the imposts of the arches and thus establishes an indissoluble link between the interior and exterior of the building. The intersection of the orders is rendered three-dimensional—i.e., this is a fully rounded system of articulation, as in similar cases where Palladio used a slender "parastatic" pilaster deriving from Vitruvius (for example, the courtyard of Palazzo Iseppo da Porto, the Villa Sarego in S. Sofia di Pedemonte, the Palazzo Giacomo Angarano, etc.).

In the side walls Palladio carved out rounded niches between the half-columns and corner pilasters (Plates 40-43), which in Bertotti Scamozzi's engraving (Fig. XIII) are filled with statues, possibly following the example of the tetrastyle entrance hall of the Villa Pisani at Montagnana where Alessandro Vittoria had been commissioned to carve figures of the Four Seasons;[81] but these statues may never have been executed, and possibly Palladio himself desired to leave the Loggia's niches empty in order to obtain a more serene chiaroscuro effect than the exterior presents, as well as one more suitable to the purposes of a portico.

The wall opposite the three arches opening onto Piazza dei Signori is adorned with a splendid, typically Palladian composition which summarizes the entire significance of the portico. In contrast to the transverse directional emphasis of the series of bays aligned along the Piazza, here the observer's attention is drawn by a perspective composition developed in depth and on axis with the central arch of the Loggia, which seems to invite one to follow the cadences of the classicizing niches and columns. Passing under an archway, which is a projection of the central exterior one but flanked by two doors with rectilinear upper frames and convex friezes instead of by niches (Plate 38), one finds oneself in a square space covered with a cross-vault and ending in an apse (Plates 44, 46). Palladio's fondness for simple spatial volumes with no architectonic articulation (except the indispensable horizontal elements which are integral parts of structures by virtue of their spatial values) is happily expressed in this feature of the building, where the apse recalls the Valmarana Chapel in Santa Corona or the sacristies of the Convento della Carità in Venice. The niche is not used to give a transverse emphasis, but is set on line with the main axis; its very position and the fact that it is the only apsidal element give it a particular significance as a terminal point, and Palladio even opened a door in it (Plates 44, 48), by simply taking the motif of the doors at either side of the archway with their rectilinear upper frames (Plate 49) and developing this motif along a curve. The transversal expansion found in the side chapels of the Chiesa del Redentore (which Palladio used primarily in the "T"-shaped halls he designed for various villas and in the designs for the "tablini" of the Carità), evidently borrowed from late-antique architecture, is found here in an entirely new form. The square space with its apse and cross-vault opens out at the sides into two smaller spaces with flat ceilings, plunged in shadow, placed beyond the coupled Tuscan columns which carry the architraves and cornices (Plates 46-47). Here again we recognize a theme which Palladio had already adopted in the past—for example, in Palazzo Chiericati. It is not so much his use of coupled columns that is significant as it is the way

in which he employed them as pauses in the rhythmic progression: they become cadences rather than supports, recalling the columns in the "in Isola" structure, employed to separate the central zone of the portico from the lateral ones.

An examination of the plan clarifies the relationship of these parts of the lower storey to the hall above, which covers only the area over the portico proper and not the square space with the apse or the two spaces flanking it which have just been described. Perhaps for this reason no particular importance has been assigned to these units, almost as if they were not to be attributed to Palladio. The above description, however, should make it obvious that Palladio's work, limited in the upper storey to the Captain's hall, must be considered in relation to an area in the lower storey of greater dimensions; this is proved by the fact that the space behind the portico has become aesthetically fused with the portico itself and is an integral part of Palladio's design. At the present stage of research and from the documents known to date, the question of the connection between Palladio's plan and the preexisting construction[82] remains an open one, especially considering the fact that later restorations and renovations have obscured this relationship still further.

According to the plan of 1571, the door in the rear niche (Plate 48) was to have opened onto a staircase leading to the upper hall, which was later replaced by the present neoclassical staircase attributed to the architect Domenico Cerato.[83] This apparently trustworthy hypothesis would support the attribution to Palladio of the end zone of the portico, for we know that he preferred not to use staircases to obtain particular spatial effects, showing, on the other hand, a strong inclination throughout his work to subordinate vertical emphases. This perhaps derives from a close loyalty to the classical tradition and to the models it furnished him. Even where the staircase has a special function to fulfill because the longitudinal wall has been suppressed (for example, in the Convento della Carità), it remains enclosed within the walls and is completely dissociated from the interplay of wall and column, rendering it an adjectival rather than a substantial element in the organization of space.[84] The staircase in the Vicentine Loggia was probably encased between walls and rectilinear in plan like those in the Palazzo Iseppo da Porto or in the plan for the town hall in Brescia;[85] if it had a different configuration the fact would have been mentioned, and greater account would have been taken of it during the neoclassical period when the stair was completely renovated in a different form.

The upper hall is entered today through the rooms of the adjacent Palazzo Trissino Baston which now serves as City Hall. It is a huge, rectangular room with a ceiling " alla ducale " (Figs. VI, XIII; Scale Drawings e, f). Although Fasolo's pictures with scenes from Roman history have been again placed in position during the most recent restoration, and the coffered ceiling has thus regained its original splendid Cinquecento form, the loss of some of the pictures formerly adorning the walls, which must have given the hall an heroic and epic atmosphere consonant with the articulation of the exterior, has greatly compromised the original character of the interior. Here—as at the villas at Maser and Caldogno, the refectory of San Giorgio, and many other Palladian buildings—the mural paintings were integrated with the architecture. In order to give free play to the cycle of paintings in the Loggia, Palladio did not hesitate to tone down the plastic quality of his work; he was content to achieve through the frescoed walls an interplay between mass and

void, between intensely luminous zones—the rectangular balconies and upper windows—and zones of illusory depth or " giuochi luministici. " For this reason, no architectonic members articulate the walls; the apertures are not emphasized, and only a horizontal band which abuts on the extrados of the arch opened in the side marks the boundary between the lower and upper registers. The latter—and also the canvases in the coffers of the ceiling—receive light from the square windows corresponding on the exterior to the pseudo-attic[86] (Fig. XIII; Plates 50-51).

However, an examination of the interior of the upper hall leads to a discussion of the problem of the original dimensions of the Loggia.

THE DIMENSIONS OF THE LOGGIA IN THE ORIGINAL PLAN

The Loggia as we know it today consists of three bays, but because construction was interrupted in 1572 and never resumed, and because the side opposite that on Via Monte di Pietà still showed in 1930 the scarfs left for future buildings, we may be sure that the structure now standing is only a part of the project; that is to say, the Loggia was intended to have had a greater number of bays than it has today. The first to have taken up this question was Francesco Muttoni, who considered that the " singolarissima fabbrica " was never meant to appear as it does today but was intended " avere sette archi per essere ridotta alla totale sua perfezione " (Fig. VI).[87] Bertotti Scamozzi, who took up the same problem, may have been influenced by some of Palladio's large Vicentine palaces (Palazzo Iseppo da Porto, Palazzo Valmarana, or Palazzo Thiene Bonin)[88] or by the imposing fragment of Palazzo Porto Breganze (which he reconstruct-

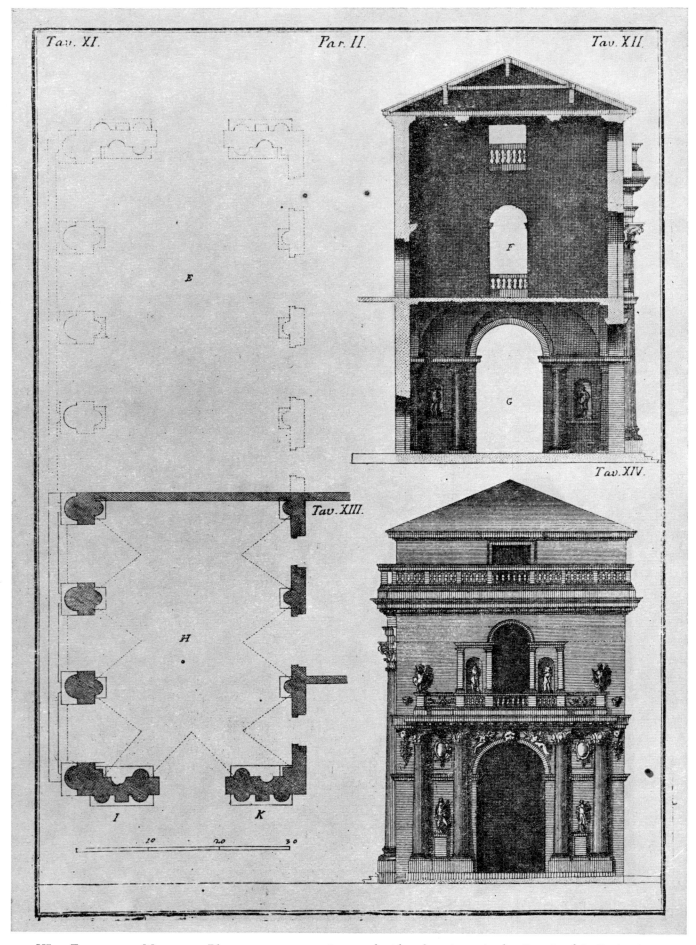

Tav. XI.   *Par. II.*   *Tav. XII.*

Tav. XIII.

Tav. XIV.

VI - FRANCESSO MUTTONI, *Plan, transverse section, and side elevation of the Loggia del Capitaniato, with a hypothetical seven-bay façade.* From *Architettura di Andrea Palladio Vicentino...*, Venice, 1760, IX, pls. XI-XIV

ed after a careful study of the foundations) when he suggested that the Loggia should also have had seven bays; this would have added four arches to the existing three, " facendo continuare lo stesso ordine d'ornamenti. " The idea that the Loggia should have had seven bays—which is a tempting one, considering the splendid engraving of the façade published by Bertotti (Figs. X-XI) [89]—no longer appears tenable if we take into consideration the exaggerated dimensions of the building, which deceptively contained only two rooms in the interior (i.e., only a loggia with portico on the ground floor and a large hall above). The proportions of the hall—as far as one can judge from all Bertotti's reconstructions—do not seem credible, for the interior seems far too long given the limited width which appears quite clearly in the section (Fig. XIII). [90] The building was probably planned to have five bays, if we follow Pane's recent assertion that the upper hall would thus have had the proper proportions of two-and-a-half squares. [91] This hypothesis finds support in one of Palladio's autograph drawings in the Vicenza museum which shows a first elaboration of the project for the Vicentine Loggia, albeit more modest in articulation. It may have been drawn about 1565, i. e., immediately after the decision had been made to renovate the original building. [92] The five bays would have stood in perfect alignment with the opposite corner of the loggia of the Basilica facing the Duomo. [93]

The drawing (Fig. III), published by Pée and Zorzi, [94] shows a succession of five round arches flanked by fluted columns corresponding to a vast hall, standing at the top of a flight of twenty-five steps (the present Loggia has only five steps). Above the entablature, with its roughly chiseled, convex frieze, rises a high attic, the rectangular windows of which are flanked by pilasters crowned with statues. In this project, as well as in the existing building, the two orders of apertures were probably intended as a purely decorative deception: they would have corresponded to a single hall which, had it been limited to the height of the lower order, would have seemed too low and contrary to all standards of proportion and function. The design shows the play of chiaroscuro not only in the fluted columns, which recall some of the London drawings, but also in the trite ornament between the capitals. The mask, [95] which Palladio adopted elsewhere as the keystone of arches, has been moved higher and functions as a bracket supporting the architrave of the entablature, which tops the whole of the lower order. Two symmetrical festoons over each arch uncoil at either side of each mask. Judging from the bay on the extreme left of the design, a slender moulding was to have linked the base of each capital to the next; this would have been carried round the corner and would have defined the horizontal zone more strongly through chiaroscuro values. The first bay on the left is adorned below the horizontal moulding with shields set into the spandrels of the arches; this motif may have been suggested by the oculi in the Basilica facing the building. The attic planned to top the Loggia is similar in the drawing to that of Palazzo Iseppo da Porto, with its terminal statues, as it appears in the design in the *Quattro Libri*; but the windows are rectangular, not square, and are flanked by lions' heads from which festoons are draped. Undue emphasis is given in this design to the attic, which is out of proportion in respect to the shafts of the columns below, as they are only a little more than twice the height of the pilasters above; moreover, it reveals certain compositional defects which come from its having been drawn too hastily, and probably it was only meant to be a suggestion. Some features may have been introduced to impress the architect's employers rather than to be actually carried out in the construction (e. g., the fluted columns and the lion's heads); they are not consistent with Palladio's own taste but are closer to that of Sansovino in their charmingly hedonistic character.[96].

As to the question of whether or not the drawing refers to the Vicentine Loggia, an affirmative answer is suggested not only by the design's character as a recognizable public-building type, but also by the fact that, although in it the façade ends at the right where a road meets it, it is accessible on the other side by means of a flight of steps which could very well have existed on the actual site of the Loggia. In other words, the building in the design seems to correspond perfectly to the Loggia's urban setting. Nevertheless the dimensions of the impressive flight of steps in front, enclosed by arms projecting from the podium (as in the Rotonda and many other of Palladio's villas),[97] would have taken too much space from the piazza and extended the Loggia too near the Basilica. We can suppose that for this reason Palladio rejected the design in favor of a less imposing flight of steps without podium arms, a solution entirely consonant with the urban layout (i. e., to the relationship of the portico to the square). We should point out, however, that the project with five bays at the head of a long flight of steps would have been an exceptionally dramatic motif and would have reproduced along the façade the effect of a proscenium from an ancient theatre. Besides the scenographic connotations, it would have formed a sort of background for civic ceremonies taking place on the flight of steps: a function quite consistent with the purpose of the Loggia, which was above all intended as a symbol of communal justice and good government.[98]

Another design with three bays, published by Zorzi,[99] has been erroneously related to the Loggia; in this case, Zorzi does not seem to have taken into consideration the fact that the three arches existing today are only part of the initial program.[100]

Just as the unfinished state of the building has constituted a challenge even from the mid-eighteenth century for the experts to define the dimensions originally planned by Palladio, it gave rise some forty years ago to a lengthy argument about the need to finish the building according to the erroneous criteria of restoration which are the cultural heritage of Viollet-le-Duc.[101] Whereas Antonio Negrin, during the last two decades of the nineteenth century, wrote of " restoring " the Loggia,[102] a little less than fifty years later, in 1926, there was talk of " completing " it. The latter was in fact resolved upon by the municipal council of Vicenza, in dedicating the building to the war dead during their session of May 5th of that year. This decision caused strong opposition among vast numbers of the more cultured sections of the population, such as the associations and societies of art and architectural historians, as well as in Milan and in the Academy in Venice.[103] All these people protested against any extension of Palladio's building which would deprive it of its " value " and " authenticity. " Despite these objections, the local authorities, together with various cultural and artistic associations who were swayed as usual by *campanilismo* and by a mistaken sense of architectural " decorum, "[104] were unanimously in favor of the completion, and the project was entrusted to the architect Ettore Fagiuoli, who accompanied his scenographic design with a long report.[105] The project, which is fully documented, provided for five bays in all (i. e., it added only two bays to those already present); the existing section was to be extended by the addition of two more bays between the Loggia and Contra' Cavour, in the Palladian style but different in form from the original ones and set further back than the Loggia itself. The lengthy attempts to justify this proposed modification—which were marked not only by the antiquated preconceptions of nineteenth-century "stilismo" but also by an excessively rhetorical style—may be passed over here. Nevertheless, it is interesting that as on previous such occasions other buildings completed after Palladio's death were introduced as examples, such as Palazzo Chiericati, the Teatro Olimpico, and, above all, the Basilica. But the lapse of centuries dividing these earlier modifications from the one now proposed, during which architecture had undergone a total revolution, were forgotten. Fagiuoli's project was approved in 1928 by the Consiglio Superiore delle Belle Arti,[106] and in 1932 the Commune of Vicenza—with undue haste and perhaps still without the complete security of the final solution—demolished the nondescript houses adjacent to the Loggia on its unfinished side (i. e., that facing Contra' Cavour; Figs. XIV-XV).[107]

As soon as these surroundings—still visible in old prints (Figs. I-II) or in photographs taken before the demolition—had been removed, a compositional problem was created in reality, which had originally been one of only an equivocal aesthetic that still had deep roots at the time. The project of completing the structure was abandoned, and a building was erected parallel to the Loggia but a little further back than the Palladian façade. The struggle between those who were courageous enough to propose a definitely modern architectural style suited to the needs of the period and those who wished to perpetuate a false period style resulted as usual

in a compromise solution which, although certainly better than the project of repeating two bays of the Palladian model, is in its " classicizing modern " style, or "simplified " classicism, a no-less vacuous and rhetorical addition. The " twentieth-century " trappings camouflaged an apartment house in front, and a shoddy Fascist assembly-hall was erected beside the Loggia. This arrangement—which still exists—was severely criticised by Giovannoni,[108] who defended the " irregular line of small, modest dwellings " (i. e., the houses adjacent to the Loggia) which he considered an indispensable element in the appearance of the monument, similar to those on Piazza delle Erbe in Verona, or in front of the Trevi Fountain,[109] or in other urban settings. In a singularly biting polemic, this important scholar firmly supported the necessity of demolishing the eyesore and erecting five new bays, identical with those of Palladio's building.[110] He recognized that by this proposal he might run the risk of being charged with inconsistency in relation to everything he had previously taught or written, but he said that it resulted from seeing the disaster of the completed project and not from a rigorous methodological position. However, even though Giovannoni suggested that the new part should be distinguished from the original by various devices, such as initials, inscriptions, and differences in decorative details like the panels flanking the windows, the result would have been equally—or perhaps even more—disappointing and the work completely useless. The " completion " of the structure would have been even more of a stylistic deception, and the whole effect would have been even less convincing.[111]

VII - Francesco Muttoni, *Side façade of the Loggia del Capitaniato.*
From *Architettura di Andrea Palladio Vicentino...*, Venice, 1760, IX, pl. XV

SELECTED CRITICISM

Although the Loggia del Capitaniato is an object of extreme interest, even a summary review of the Palladian literature [112] reveals that it has been the least studied of all the certain works by the architect. Many essays dealing with his activity fail even to mention the Loggia, or else refer to it only fleetingly. This lapse is completely justified in Anton Francesco Doni's [113] little volume, since it appeared more than fifteen years before work on the Loggia had been started (i. e., shortly after Vasari's "Lives of the Painters"). [114] However, there is no mention of the Loggia in the oldest biography of Palladio that we possess, which was written about 1615 by Paolo Gualdo; [115] it is invaluable for its biographical information, but it contains almost no references to the architect's works.

Temanza's splendid volume, published shortly after the middle of the eighteenth century, [116] marks a renewal of interest in the Veneto in Palladio's work, following the abovementioned dissemination of Palladian motifs in England. But even Temanza failed to mention the Loggia, despite the extensiveness of his work. His suggestion that systematic plans and surveys should be made of Palladio's work was taken up in a partial and loose way by Muttoni and later found its real executor in Ottavio Bertotti Scamozzi.

Barbieri gives a thorough account of Bertotti's work, [117] and it is necessary here to mention only his short guidebook to the monuments and works of art in Vicenza published in 1761. Following a style much in vogue at the time, this is written in the form of a dialogue between a certain " signor Leandro vicentino," who acts as cicerone, and " un signor Guglielmo, inglese,

uomo dabbene e innamorato dell'Italia." [118] A brief examination of the Loggia is included in this short essay, accompanied by elevations (Figs. VIII-IX). [119] Bertotti Scamozzi anticipates considerations that were to be taken up some fifteen years later in his large and well-known study of Palladio's buildings, favoring a strict adherence to the neoclassical aesthetic. Any hint of liberties taken with the established canons disturbs him, and he condemns them as errors or as inadmissible " improprieties." In fact, he seems almost to echo Muttoni, for he expresses an extremely reserved opinion on the entablature cut by the windows: William remarks that he finds a great license in the building, and Leander hastens to excuse Palladio on the grounds that he was unable to control the execution of his design. [120]

Bertotti's long description accompanying the splendid engraving of the Loggia published in his *Fabbriche e disegni* (Figs. X-XIII) contains other observations relating to presumed lapses in syntax: for example, the balconies supported by modillions projecting in front of the windows and the balustrade above the cornice of the main order seem to be solutions contrary to the laws of apparent and real stability. For once Bertotti tried to limit the extent of criticism that these departures from the established canons might seem to justify: " Ma tali obiezioni non hanno grande peso; che, per essere le finestre frapposte tra grosse colonne, se i loro poggiuoli fossero ritirati, frustranei riuscirebbero intieramente a chi si volesse affacciare per vedere la piazza da ogni parte. Riguardo poi alla balaustrata, non deve sembrar troppo ardita, perch'essa intieramente non pesa sopra l'aggetto della cornice ma riposa in qual-che maniera sul vivo. Non può negarsi per altro, che il gran Maestro accostumato non era a seguir questa pratica; ma la ne-cessità delle circostanze, nel caso di cui parliamo, sarebbe stata una sufficiente ra-gione per abbracciarla." [121]

We have already mentioned the cautious proposal to carry out an " ideal recon-struction " of the Loggia put forward by Bertotti, and we might add that his engrav-ings are not only invaluable in the aesthetic sense,[122] but they also permit us to elimi-nate the numerous abovementioned altera-tions introduced by Muttoni into his plan of the Loggia (Fig. IV).[123] Although Ber-totti scrupulously listed all the "variations" Muttoni had inserted, publishing a plan which corresponds completely with the actual structure and therefore is some dis-tance from Muttoni's, he does not con-demn his predecessor's plans as we might legitimately have expected of him. Bertotti Scamozzi himself had also expressed some doubts regarding Palladio's work, again in the name of neoclassical taste: " La serie di queste disparità dipendenti, come può credersi, da inavvertenza degli assistenti di quell'Architetto come dall'una parte esclu-de, mediante l'infedeltà de' disegni, il mag-gior bene che poteva produrre un'opera ben concepita e dispendiosa, così indicava, dall'altra, necessità di una produzione più corretta, la quale dando le mirabili opere Palladiane misurate colla possibile preci-sione, ben potesse servire di non fallace argomento agli studi degli architetti."

Milizia's book on Palladio's work expres-ses the same reservations.[124] In his opinion Palladio was the greatest architect since the age of Augustus, one who always had antiquity as a model but who nonetheless was not exempt from " errors."

We may refer the reader to what has already been written concerning this neo-classical critic's opinion of Palladio,[125] and it is necessary to emphasize here only the curious contradiction between the praise he lavishes on the Vicentine architect at the beginning and end of his essay, and the largely negative judgment, based on the presupposition of a type of perfection known only to himself, that he pronounces in the course of the essay itself. It is indeed strange that such a summary man-ner of dispensing with Palladio's activity (" egli non ebbe che un barlume di bello architettonico, né giunse a veder chiara la origine della sua professione ") should have been so common, recurring continuously throughout the nineteenth century. This may be explained by the fact that Milizia is the most authoritative exponent of the neoclassical aesthetic; he was not only the real cultural heir to Lodoli's rationalistic principles but was also the propagator of Winckelmann's and Mengs's theories of architecture.

An echo of Milizia—who does not even mention the Loggia, leaving it out of his list of Palladio's Vicentine buildings [126]— may be found at the beginning of the nine-teenth century in a lecture given in 1810 before the Accademia Veneta di Belle Arti by its president, Leopoldo Cicognara.[127] Notwithstanding the eulogistic tone of the talk, the Ferrarese historian asserts, among other things, that: " Nè a Palladio pos-sonsi attribuire alcune scorrezioni, che si rivelano in parecchie opere del suo stile, delle quali non sono incolpabili che gli ese-cutori, allontanati da' suoi modelli, e con-tinuando con mediocre dottrina le opere da lui cominciate e rimaste imperfette." Milizia had attributed some " errors " to the builders because they were not conso-nant with Palladio's own principles, but considered others to be the architect's own, because " after all, he was only human." Cicognara expresses greater freedom in his criticism when he observes that: " [Pal-ladio] non fu invariabile nelle modulazioni

VIII - OTTAVIO BERTOTTI SCAMOZZI, *Front elevation of the Loggia del Capitaniato.* From *Il forestiere istrutto nelle cose più rare di Architettura e di alcune pitture della città di Vicenza*, Vicenza, 1780, pl. II

degli ordini, ma a seconda dei vari generi degli edifici v'introdusse le più applaudite modificazioni; siccome lo stesso fece delle proporzioni, spesso determinandosi in ragion composta dell'Aritmetica, della Geometria, e dell'Armonia, secondo che vide essersi ciò praticato ancor dagli antichi." Although the Loggia del Capitaniato is not mentioned in the short review he gave of

Palladio's works in his lecture,[128] the general considerations mentioned above concern the building, albeit indirectly.

Similarly, although there is no reference to the Loggia in Galeani Napione's biography of Palladio written a few years later,[129] it is appropriate to quote that author's acute critical appreciation of the relationship between the architect and the antique:

"Anche di Grecia trasse egli disegni (il che non fece con inscrupolosa e fredda esattezza geometrica, ma con fantasia vivace e propria di chi aveva imbevuta la mente... delle grandiose idee degli antichi...), da pochi ruderi, dai laceri avanzi e dalle semplici descrizioni di Vitruvio...."[130] Galeani Napione admiringly regards Palladio as the last upholder of the Renaissance tradition and as clearly antithetical to the new proto-Baroque tendencies that were beginning to appear on the Italian architectural scene: "Nell'ornato poi degli edifizi, che un valent'uomo dice a buona ragione lo scoglio dell'architettura, solenne e sovrano maestro è il Palladio, lontano da quelle licenze cui aprì la strada Michelangelo, e che dal Borromini e dal Guarini vennero spinte all'estremo...."[131] This is an interpretation which a decade later was to be less radically formulated in Quatremère de Quincy's cautious judgment of Palladio's style, which followed a middle path between the severe, systematic canons of the classicists and the excessive licence of those who wanted to overthrow all rules.[132]

The Loggia is only mentioned as a "palazzo delegatizio," with no indication of its date, in the list of Palladio's Vicentine works accompanying an essay on the architect and on Scamozzi written by Filippo Scolari in 1837.[133] This essay mentions another "Palazzo del Capitanio" in the Piazza dei Signori in Padua, which was at that time attributed to Palladio, perhaps because it was confused with the one in Vicenza; but Scolari denied the "common opinion" and pointed out that the frieze of the Paduan building bore the date 1607 for the cornerstone laying and 1612 for the completion of the structure, both dates well after Palladio's death. It is worth remarking that in his discussion of Palladio's personality the author declares[134] that Milizia had often wrongly delighted in attacking him. It is too bad that such a clear op-

position to the opinions of the neoclassical theorist is not matched in the essay by an exact critical definition of Palladio's role as an architect; all Scolari's opinions are obscured by the usual vague expressions to which we have become accustomed: "Lo studio e l'amore dell'Antichità non andarono mai scompagnati in Palladio dall'osservazione più attenta e sagace di ciò, che poteva convenire ai costumi del tempo, ed all'avanzamento vero dell'arte. Per ciò conobbe il bisogno di lavorare di nuovo sullo studio degli ordini, nelle cui proporzioni e modanature (combinate colle viste della solidità e della convenienza nel tutto e nelle parti degli edifizi ai quali si applicano) consiste la ragione vera e l'efficacia dell'arte." Thus, in his opinion an elegant simplicity characterises Palladio's work, and in order to achieve it the architect took care not to break up the orders into too great an elaborateness. After having emphasised the "majesty, order, proportion, suitability, variety, unity, and solidity" of Palladio's work, Scolari states that: "È soltanto nelle sue opere scritte che l'intelletto può scorgere qualche cosa che, dopo aver veduta una fabbrica di Palladio, lo possa far amare ed ammirare ancor più." Implicit reservations, however, seem almost to mitigate his previous enthusiasm for Palladio in the passage in which the architect is accused of having yielded too much to the wishes of his patrons.[135]

About the middle of the last century, Abbot Antonio Magrini completed a profound study of the Loggia,[136] in which appears a long, detailed, and very accurate biography of Palladio based on new research in the archives. Magrini is rather cautious in his critical judgments, and his large volume is difficult to consult because there are no chapter-divisions or indices and because he fails to emphasize the significant points among the mass of details he has assembled.

Magrini publishes the deliberations of the municipal council (discussed above) concerning the allotment of funds for the construction of the Loggia from documents in the city archives, which have been republished by Zorzi, after a careful check against the originals.[137] In his discussion of problems concerning the Loggia, Magrini merely points out the impossibility of attributing to the builders the serious license on both façades of cutting the architrave by the windows (Plates 10-11), as Bertotti Scamozzi had done: not because he is convinced that Palladio was in Vicenza during the construction of the building (which has been definitely disproved[138]), but because a similarly arbitrary feature can be found in another certain work by Palladio, the Villa Barbaro at Maser, and is even published in the *Quattro Libri*.[139] This is a rather acute observation, as Magrini recognizes the use of the same device (albeit in a different form) in both buildings; it was intended to lend a dramatic character alien to the serene classicism of the youthful works. However, he fails to draw any precise conclusions from this; he merely notes the fact and formulates a vague doubt that the patrons' intervention would have forced this choice on the architect,[140] a doubt which is both unjustified and unacceptable, as we have noted above. In conclusion, Magrini writes: " Ch'egli abbia consentita la licenza di un architrave spezzato io nol dirò, né so se fosse bastante scusa una di quelle che egli ha pur deplorato, di essersi dovuto accomodare alla volontà dei padroni, o alle necessità del sito, che in questo caso presentava vecchie impalcature di adiacente edificio da pareggiarsi in elevazione."[141] But not even the preexisting structures or the "liberties" Palladio freely introduced into his work by virtue of his poetical imagination seem sufficient to explain the change of rhythm.

During the second half of the nineteenth century many historico-critical essays were published on Palladio. Referring to only the more important of them, the Loggia is not mentioned by Boito,[142] Lampertico,[143] or Biàdego;[144] Zanella,[145] the author of a biography of Palladio published in 1880 (and motivated solely by the desire to honor Vicenza's most distinguished citizen[146]), refers to it only briefly, and neither the new edition of Castellini[147] nor Bortolan's essay[148] adds anything new to previous studies. Burckhardt refers to the Loggia in his *Cicerone*, which had appeared a few years previously in 1855 and in which many pages deal with the architecture of the Renaissance.[149] But whereas he was the first—if not the only—critic to approach Palladio with a Goethe-like freedom of spirit, according to Pane,[150] recognizing that in his buildings Palladio followed nothing except the order and sentiment of the proportions, his opinion of the Loggia seems hasty and unacceptable and follows Milizia's lines. He considers that in the Loggia Palladio was wrong to apply his monumental forms to a structure of small dimensions, problems of this nature having been more satisfactorily resolved during the Quattrocento. But the architect seemed to have realized his error, as on the lateral façade he carried the columns only up to the height of the lower storey and treated this whole façade in a more decorative sense.

Despite an increasing interest in Palladio's work, which in this century has caused an ever-accelerating number of attempts to achieve a critical precision both about his personality and in research into his individual works, it cannot be said that—from the critical point of view—the field has been quickly freed from equivocal aesthetic viewpoints. The character of Palladio's work has perhaps favored such equivocation, for as one critic happily put it, " Esprime la vera classicità nell'apparenza del classicismo."[151] For example, Fletcher's monograph on Palladio, published in 1902, repeats word for word Muttoni's and Bertotti Scamozzi's purist interpretation of the "defect" of the windows that cut unjustifiably into the architrave.[152] No explanation is given concerning the change in rhythm between the front and side façades (Plate 4), and the author contents himself with recording that the motif of the arch between two niches which are flanked by Doric pilasters, topped by architraves, and contain statues (i.e., the Serliana) is echoed in English neoclassical architecture, especially in the work of the Adam brothers.[153]

Anderson's position a few years later in his book on Italian Renaissance architecture is somewhat similar:[154] although he considers the Loggia an interesting and handsome edifice and not lacking in originality, the break in the architrave (a sign of decadence) disturbs him considerably, as does the use of triglyphs as supports.[155] Although not explicitly, he interprets these details as traces of mannerism and as forerunners of the new Baroque taste.[156] The theory that Palladio was an initiator of the Baroque style rather than the last representative of the Renaissance was taken up again in 1919 in Brinckmann's well-known book.[157]

Gurlitt,[158] in his standard treatment of Palladio's work, is even more awkwardly equivocal when he states, for example, that artistic form predominates over practicality in the architect's buildings, and beauty over the expression of function. But it is unnecessary here to dwell further on the errors inherent in such a narrow interpretation, since Gurlitt does not mention the Loggia.[159]

During the first three decades of this century, Ricci's summary and schematic treatise on Cinquecento architecture[160]—in which one reads that Palladio, as the heir to the precepts of Brunelleschi and Bra-

mante, suceeded in giving a "genteel renewal" to antique styles—and Loukomski's monograph[161]—which wastes few words on the Loggia—were published. Although Loukomski points out "l'impression d'inachevé" which the building makes upon the observer and emphasizes the lavish chiaroscuro effects of the stuccoes set between the columns, he does not adopt the puristic reservations usual with earlier writers.[162] In discussing the character of Palladian architecture, he offers a rather schematic but substantially acceptable interpretation: in his opinion, the ingenious Palladio knew how to recover the classical purity which his own period had lost—i.e., he was heir to the Renaissance tradition but did not allow a rigid or unintelligent interpretation of the canons to produce sterility.[163]

Loukomski's observations, intelligent though they may be, are apparently not echoed in the monograph by Melani,[164] which need be mentioned here only as a negative example of the perpetuation of the errors of neoclassical purism, produced in a period when that taste can no longer be justified. His remarks may otherwise be passed over as devoid of any critical acumen.

In the same year (1928) the Roumanian critic Cantacuzène considered Palladio to be far too literary and archaeological, because his nostalgic attitude to the past led him to adopt antique forms derived from the classicist tradition.[165] Although this view is diametrically opposed to that of the neoclassical critics, it is nevertheless equally erroneous; still, Cantacuzène does acknowledge Palladio's independence of contemporary currents and his isolated position as an artist, similar to that of Michelangelo: "Entre le dôme de Florence bâti par Brunelleschi (où le sens gothique de la construction à nervure cherche à résoudre le problème du Panthéon d'Agrippa) et le dôme de la Salute de Longhena, oeuvre d'une virtuosité sans lendemain,

IX - OTTAVIO BERTOTTI SCAMOZZI, *Side elevation of the Loggia del Capitaniato.* From *Il forestiere istrutto nelle cose più rare di Architettura e di alcune pitture della città di Vicenza*, Vicenza, 1780, pl. III

entre ces deux pôles de la Renaissance si dissemblables dans leur parenté, Palladio prend une place d'astre fixe, étranger et indifférent aux constellations." Fundamental to the expression of Palladio's genius was the Vicentine milieu, with its freedom from prejudices: " une société impatiente de rivaliser avec les autres villes d'Italie, et prête à mettre ses moyens à la disposition de celui qui saurait réaliser son idéal." Concerning the façades of Palladio's buildings, Cantacuzène discerns in them, together with a nostalgia for the antique (" l'élément intellectuel gouvernant les idées de Palladio "), an architectonic concentration, " quelque chose de serré, de condensé, une sorte de puissance non développée, un surplus de vie par rapport aux formes." [166]

In 1930 Argan took up the problem of the connection between Palladio and neoclassicism,[167] which was to be treated later by Brandi.[168] After pointing out an equivocation recurring in histories of architecture—that of considering Palladio as an exponent of severe accuracy in using the canons, as frigidly and pedantically erudite as if he were a neoclassicist—he discusses the distance between Palladio's concepts and those of the neoclassicists, which is manifest in the "bizzarie" Milizia condemns so harshly: i.e., in the lack of a rigid application of the canons in Palladio's works (such as the use of a composite order above a rusticated base, or a combination of large and small pilasters rising from the same level).[169] The position of architectural elements from Roman precepts used in quite different spatial arrangements disturbed Milizia, for (as Argan has pointed out) in this way Palladio caused these elements to lose all spatial significance, whereas according to the grammar of the purists they had a precise space-defining task. To this extent Palladio was completely independent of both the taste for the antique

and the Roman Renaissance, for by adhering to the figurative culture of the Cinquecento he created a chiaroscuro whose function was no longer to indicate relief, but purely to form chromatic contrast. For " space as depth " Palladio substituted the plane as absolute frontality, as a negation of perspective and as a sudden emergence of spatial elements to the surface in an affirmative chromatic resolution. The possibility of juxtaposing two architectonic forms rising from the same plane like two shades of color allows Argan to assert that Palladio became a pure decorator,[170] by virtue of that "senso della decorazione immediata" which Burger called the "Magie der Darstellungkünste." [171] One emphasizes in this way the decorative and chromatic elements sought by Palladio, who profited from variations in the intensity of light,[172] enabling us to establish a parallel between his approach and that of Paolo Veronese: a parallel in which Brizio has stressed the use of chromatic values and the sense of pure decoration.[173] The main effect at which Palladio aimed was the juxtaposition of the minimum and maximum intensities of light from black to white, including all the intermediate shades as pure chromatic units. However, we must recognize that Palladio, dedicating himself only to architecture, was better able than anyone else to create in his buildings a synthesis of plastic and spatial values with those which are more properly chromatic, as demonstrated in the above description of the Loggia.

Recently Argan, in a discussion of Palladio's artistic formation and the character of his work, has pointed out how in the latter a new "non-perspective" relationship is established between building and surroundings. Insisting on the "non-perspective" nature of Palladio's architecture, Argan states that because of this very characteristic such architecture cannot be con-

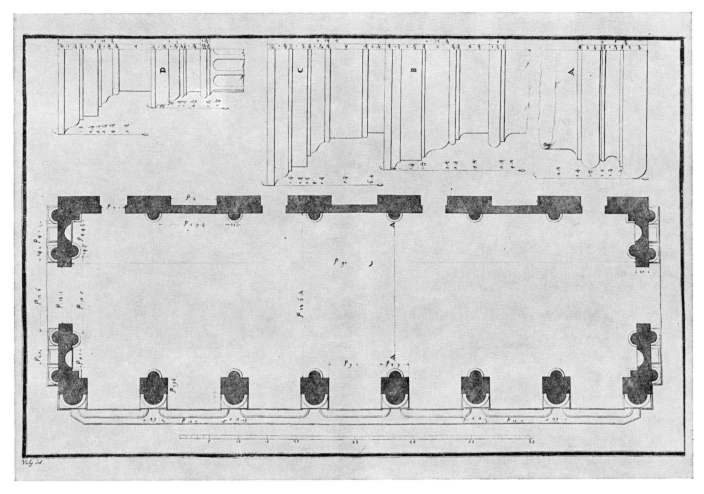

X - OTTAVIO BERTOTTI SCAMOZZI, *Plan of the Loggia del Capitaniato with a hypothetical seven-bay façade.*
From *Le fabbriche e i disegni di Andrea Palladio...*, Vicenza, 1776, I, pl. XIII

sidered " spatial." [174] Pane, however, is inclined to reject the proposed antithesis between perspective and spatial qualities because he considers them to be interdependent and indivisible in plastic vision,[175] and thus he does not accept Argan's theory.[176]

The studies which appeared during the third decade of this century are less interesting. Willich's is merely philological and bibliographical,[177] and Giovannoni hardly mentions the Loggia.[178] Giovannoni had already classified Palladio in the late Renaissance tradition as one who followed the models of the past, erecting "bare" and "cold" structures.[179] The terms he applies to Palladio's work are general ones of symmetry, harmonious regularity, perfect proportion, application of the classical elements, etc.; although he devotes insufficient attention to defining the architect's personality, his opinions show that he is inclined to consider him as little more than an academic (placing him in the same current as Vignola), opposed to the tendency to transform traditional elements personified by Michelangelo, who set out resolutely in search of a new style. An interpretation of this sort is easily rejected because it fails to recognise Palladio's most special quality, that of being an independent creator of forms. It seems clear that a judgment of this nature limits itself to considering only the most apparent or exterior aspects of Palladio's work, at the expense of the essence of his art.

No less general and literary are the observations formulated by Adolfo Venturi in the monograph on Palladio which is part of his monumental history of Italian art,[180] where he writes of the Loggia that its motifs are the same as those of Palazzo Valmarana, but translated into terms of mass, in a "romantic exaltation" of chiaroscuro contrasts.[181] He emphasizes effects which are entirely new and unusual in Palladio: the massive balconies which rest their weight on ponderous consoles, the ornamental exuberance which causes the arches of the lower order almost to disappear, and the weight which seems to shorten and compress the spaces between columns. On the side of the Loggia, Palladio turns into a scenographer, offering a variation on the bold *sottinsù* view which Argan has called the fundamental *trait d'union* between the poetic vision of Palladio and that of Veronese.[182] After pointing out the accentuation of chiaroscuro and the projecting members of the articulation, Venturi concludes that this is the richest in pathos of all Palladio's works, as it looms up "obscured by shadows like a Piranesi ruin," an allusion to the dramatic character of the chiaroscuro effects.[183]

This very peculiarity—the Loggia's vibrant chiaroscuro, obtained by devices like the repeated and full use of stucco, the window frames cutting into the architrave, and the triglyph-modillions jutting out below the balconies—has induced a great many critics to formulate a different interpretation of Palladio, considering him a "mannerist" and pointing out the connections and relationships between his production and contemporary work in the new mode which was then diffusing itself in northern Italy.

Without ever having left his native town, Palladio was in contact with Serlio at Vicenza in 1539, with Sanmicheli in 1541 and 1542, and with Giulio Romano in the same year, for they had all been summoned by the Consiglio dei Cento to discuss the problem of restoring the Basilica.[184] As a guest with Trissino of Cornaro he had seen Falconetto's work in Padua between 1538 and 1540.[185] In Vicenza itself he had watched Bartolomeo Ammannati at work, as he was called to construct a scenographic fountain (later destroyed) in the garden of the Gualdo family at Pusterla.[186]

The thesis that Palladio was a mannerist —first proposed by Michalski[187] and Becherucci[188] some thirty years ago and taken up by Pevsner,[189] Wittkower,[190] Chastel,[191] Bettini,[192] and others more recently—transfers historical considerations such as contacts between artists onto an unacceptable level of artistic evaluation; it seems, in fact, not to take account of the significance of the term "mannerist," which is too limited. Even if the latter is meant as a fully positive term (as Pallucchini has suggested,[193] followed by Tafuri[194]), like every other schematic definition and every "ism" it is still totally inadequate to define the poetic complex of Palladio.[195] The rediscovery of Mannerism due to the two major contemporary currents of Expressionism and Surrealism has thrown light on a phenomenon closely connected with Cinquecento classicism, but nevertheless distinct from it. The limitation of Mannerism has been properly defined in a lack of courage, in a kind of revolutionary commitment which was only partial, as if it actually wanted to be "anti-Renaissance."[196] Although Pevsner has recently insisted on the evidence of mannerist traits in Palladio's work, which show a fondness on the artist's part for the ambiguities of this style particularly evident around 1560-70, he is nevertheless obliged to recognize that such traits never predominate in his work.[197] This seems obviously to contradict his previous statement that Palladio, like Veronese, was a Renaissance artist, but that no artist can set himself against his century, meaning that insofar as Palladio participated in the culture of his age he could not reject the mannerist elements

XI - OTTAVIO BERTOTTI SCAMOZZI, *Front elevation of the Loggia del Capitaniato, with a hypothetical seven-bay façade.* From *Le fabbriche e i disegni di Andrea Palladio...*, Vicenza, 1776, I, pl. XIV

diffused throughout the Veneto at that time.

Ackerman's position is closer to the present writer's: [198] having recognized the anti-classical spirit of Palladio's later work, he also held that he was independent of mannerist culture. We should not speak of ambiguity or mannerist fantasy in connection with Palladio so much as of what we might call "pictorialism" ("pittoricismo"); we should see Palladio as representing a link between the Roman tradition and the attitude prevailing in the Veneto, which is well represented in the two opposite façades of the Villa Malcontenta.

Ackerman criticizes the excessive use of stucco ornament in Palladio's buildings and points out that in his drawings and published designs the ornamentation is much simpler and more subdued. The stuccoes adorning the Loggia seem out of scale to him, and in general he maintains that

the iconography was not under Palladio's direct control, which weakens the tectonic vigor.[199] The reduced amount of stucco and other ornamentation in the illustrations to the *Quattro Libri* is due to the simplification required for the woodcut technique, and in his drawings Palladio aimed at a final synthesis; but we cannot agree with Ackerman's final statement that the sculpture in Palladio's work is an integral part of the architecture, albeit differing in quality according to the sculptors employed, and that it represents a chromatic element which is Palladio's way of showing that he felt himself to be a participant in the culture of the Veneto. We must agree instead with Blunt,[200] who insists that "... Palladio, ... whose methods had much in common with the classical architects of the beginning of the sixteenth century, relied more on his study of the [antique] buildings themselves than on the rules of

Vitruvius; Serlio, on the other hand, ... pins all his faith on the latter." [201]

Zevi has recently emphasized Palladio's link with Mannerism in a particular way, relating it to his contacts during his twenties and thirties with artists frequenting Pedemuro's atelier, who had trained in Rome under the influence of Bramante and then emigrated to northern Italy after the disaster of 1527.[202] Palladio's contacts with them were frequent, and to these contacts one might add the opportunity which he had to know the works of Michelangelo, Antonio da Sangallo, and Pirro Ligorio during his trips to Rome in 1541, 1546, 1547, and 1549.[203] Zevi insists on the "ardor of spirit" of Palladio's expression, which is "equally removed from the classical structures of antiquity and from the perspective systems characteristic of the Renaissance," and on his state of "profound anxiety" or "cultural alienation." He concludes that: "Palladio... was not a mannerist in a categorical or strictly historical sense. However, from his youth he was certainly aware of the conflicts and distress of the great sixteenth-century crisis, and he assimilated these as conscious aspects of his own development." He sees the Loggia as "testimony of a senile anticlassical rage" which led Palladio to a "paradoxical degree of formlessness." These observations, interesting for the psychological penetration they betray, do not preclude (as the author himself states) that "a psychological and moral impasse, rather than an artistic one, separated Palladio from every other architect of his time";[204] thus he confirms Palladio's originality, as we emphasized in the foregoing pages, although from a different standpoint.

Zevi has pointed out the formal crisis of Palladio's late period[205] and has suggested that it is inseparable from the sociological milieu of Venice. Commenting on this, Pane states that events defining the political and economic crisis in Venetian society during Palladio's lifetime did not impede the development of a splendid figurative culture; thus the formal crisis in Palladio's later works must be understood as the result of his own natural development, which was directed toward injecting new life into a declining architectural tradition.[206]

In conclusion, let us affirm that, although some mannerist traits derived from Serlio and Giulio Romano are recognizable in Palladio's work, an analysis of his production shows a development of such coherence that it appears as a single work, and, at the same time, his architectonic poetry transcends all cultural sources, whether "academic" or "mannerist."[207] In other words, as Pane made clear, one must not seek to consider Palladio the product of Mannerism but to recognize in him— as one does with every great creator of form—an independent and personal formation and experience attained through a systematic rediscovery of the ancient world, to which he came late compared to others of his time and without being aware of the crisis already evident.[208] We must avoid rigid schemes of critical judgment and attempts to label this grand and solitary Vicentine genius, who attained the highest mode of expression after a humble apprenticeship as a stonecutter through having applied himself to the study of Roman antiquities; thus we will recognize in Palladio an expressive liberty, which was a personal thing and was not derived from the mannerist culture or from the classicizing formulae into which he constantly infused new life. We can rescue the Loggia del Capitaniato from all negative criticism, realizing that it is a perfectly completed statement, and agree with Pallucchini that here also "il capriccio si esprime come evasione lirica."[209]

b) - Loggia del Capitaniato: façade facing Piazza dei Signori (before 1932)

NOTES

[1] PÉE, 1941, p. 140, places the residence of the Vicentine captain about 1343 in houses belonging to the Verlato. ZORZI, 1965 (I), pp. 109 ff., affirms that this can be verified from 1374 on.

[2] The remains of a tower forming part of the Verlato palace is still partly visible behind the present-day Loggia, in Via del Monte di Pietà. PÉE, 1941, cites two documents dated 1374 and 1404 in which the palace is indicated as the captain's residence; he states that the first mention of the Loggia occurs in 1399, whereas MAGRINI, 1845-46, pp. 162-163, writes that it appears in the Vicentine archives from 1410. BORTOLAN, 1892, also furnishes some information on Palladio's work.

[3] The former already existed at the beginning of the thirteenth century and was used for the administration of justice; the latter was erected in 1222-23. Remains of these palaces may be seen in the Arch of the Zavatteri at the eastern corner of the present-day Basilica; however, the area was used in 1444 for the construction of a new Palazzo della Ragione by Domenico da Venezia, replacing the earlier buildings which had been damaged by fire on various occasions.

[4] Concerning the Vicentine Basilica, restored by Palladio in 1549 following a wooden model made in 1546, see PANE, 1961 (I), pp. 143-148 and passim, and BARBIERI, 1970. Palladio enclosed the Gothic structure in Renaissance arcades.

[5] The Torre dei Bissari, erected in the twelfth century, became municipal property sometime during the first thirty years of the following century. The upper part was extended up to the bell-chamber with its arcuated *bifore* in 1311 and was completed in 1444 with octagonal orders diminishing up to the pinnacle. The portal in the base is by Giovanni da Pedemuro (1530).

[6] ZORZI, 1965 (I), p. 109, figs. 79-81, affirms that the appearance of the old Loggia may be reconstructed from the two lateral tondi on a gilded cassone with allegorical themes by Bartolomeo Montagna and from a cassone panel, also by Montagna, representing St. Paul (Museo Poldi Pezzoli, Milan; no. 119). PÉE, although admitting that it is impossible to reconstruct the actual form of the original Loggia, mistakenly cites among works that show buildings of this type in the background a *Noli me tangere* by Montagna (Kaiser Friedrich Museum, Berlin; no. 44b) and an engraving by Montagna's son Benedetto representing St. Jerome (B. XIII. 340. 14). Since we have no precise points of reference for the urban setting, the interpretation of the first two scenes becomes problematical, while the reference to the two other scenes, in which the Vicentine Loggia does not appear at all, is irrelevant. CEVESE, 1964, pp. 334, is therefore right when he points out that these representations are of a generic kind and can in no way be applied to the Loggia del Capitaniato.

[7] On Fra' Giocondo, see VASARI, 1880; THIEME-BECKER, 1921, pp. 64-68. The loggia of the Council of Verona was built between 1476 and 1491. Documents record the names of the builders (Daniele della Banda and others), but not the name of the architect. VENTURI, 1924, p. 589, does not connect the name of the Veronese friar with this work. FIOCCO, 1915, 1916, and 1933 (II), col. 159, holds a contrary opinion. Although it is unnecessary in this case to refer to types, it should be remembered that public arcades were already typical of medieval cities and were used for discussing politics and business affairs. In addition to the numerous merchants' arcades named after the corporations to which they belonged, we may recall among the chief loggias existing prior to Palladio's time the Loggia della Signoria (later Loggia dei Lanzi) in Florence, built between 1376 and 1391 as the place of installation for elected officials; the Loggia Fortebraccio in Perugia (1423); the Loggia del Papa in Siena (1462); and the Loggetta di San Marco in Venice, built by Jacopo Sansovino (1537-40), which was at first an assembly-place for the nobles and after 1569 became the residence of the three procurators commanding the armed guard of the Doge's Palace. Later examples are the Loggia dei Banchi in Genoa (1570-95) and that of the market in Pisa (1603-5). In discussing types of Italian communal loggias, ACKERMAN, 1966, p. 120, points out the important difference between those built as simple vaulted canopies, such as the Loggia dei Lanzi or the Loggetta di S. Marco, and those in which a first-storey hall erected above an arched portico was used for assemblies or as the residence of the highest magistrate in the city (cf. examples in Milan, Brescia, Verona, Pistoia, and Vicenza). Mention should also be made of the Loggia Cornaro in Padua, built in 1524 by Falconetto and known to Palladio; see ZORZI, 1965 (I), p. 115. On the work of this Paduan architect, see BROSCH, 1935, pp. 5-7; BRENZONI, 1953-54, pp. 269-296; SEMENZATO, 1961, pp. 70-77; BOLZONELLA, 1962, pp. 40-41; FORSSMAN, 1966, pp. 52-67.

[8] See PANE, 1961 (I), pp. 43-44.

[9] See PÉE, 1941, p. 142, who speaks only of the Maestro Giovanni known as the young Palladio's master.

[10] See ZORZI, 1925, pp. 37 ff. Lo Scarpagnino was to make a second trip to Vicenza in 1525, "pro reparatione palatii"; see PANE, 1961 (I), p. 16.

[11] Whereas ZORZI, 1965 (I), p. 109, attributes to Francesco Vecellio the fresco depicting the Judgment of Solomon, PÉE, 1941, p. 142, gives it to Titian; Titian's brother Francesco would have collaborated with his pupils Gregorio and Bartolomeo in painting the ceiling decoration, the subject of which is not known. The Noah scene was painted by Paris Bordone; see CANOVA, 1961, pp. 77-88.

[12] ZORZI, 1965 (I), p. 109.

[13] PÉE, 1941, p. 142. A druggist's shop once existed on the ground floor, beneath the Loggia. Cf. the Archivio Notarile di Vicenza: notary Bortolo Piacentini, 2 January 1544. The series of repairs are also recorded by BORTOLAN, 1892, and by ZORZI, 1965 (I), p. 110 and n. 4.

[14] Concerning the ruined condition of the building, see MAGRINI, 1845-46, pp. 163 ff.

[15] See ACKERMAN, 1966, p. 120, and MAGRINI, 1845-46, p. 163, who publishes the deliberations of the "Consiglio dei deputati" of 31 January 1565 (*Libri Partium*, Archivio di Torre, Vicenza, Biblioteca Bertoliana, III, p. 354). See also ZORZI, 1965 (I), p. 110 and pp. 117-118, doc. I; Zorzi transcribed anew all the documents from the archives, which had been less accurately published by Magrini.

[16] See MAGRINI, 1845-46, pp. 163-164, who publishes the Council's deliberation, approved on 18 April 1571 (Archivio di Torre, *Libro Parti*, II, 572 t.). Payment was made on 23 April 1571; see ZORZI, 1965 (I), p. 110 and p. 118, docs. 2 and 3. The sum of 25 ducats was detracted because it had already been paid to Valerio Barbarano di Saraceno for expenses sustained in repairing the roof of the old Loggia.

[17] See MAGRINI, 1845-46, pp. 163-164; on 8 August 1571 another document records that a further payment of 266 troni 13 marchetti was made for the Loggia; see ZORZI, 1965 (I), p. 118, doc. 4 (Archivio di Torre, *Libro Provisioni*, XIII, p. 129).

[18] See ZORZI, 1965 (I), p. 111. The author records (n. 12)

that on 17 February 1571 Palladio received a payment of 10 gold scudi as an advance on his salary for the months of July and August for supervising the work being carried out on the Basilica's loggias (Archivio di Torre, *Libro Provisioni*, XII, app. p. 76).

[19] See MAGRINI, 1845-46, p. 164.

[20] The minutes of the council meeting of 28 November 1571 are published by MAGRINI, 1845-46, p. 165.

[21] See the deliberations of the council of 23 December 1571 (*Libro Parti*, II, p. 592) published by MAGRINI, 1845-46, pp. 165-166. The interpretation of this act seems clear enough: the 300 ducats requested were granted, but it was established that other funds would not be forthcoming. PÉE is therefore inaccurate when he writes (1941, p. 143) that on 23 December it was reported to the council that the major part of the structure was built but that another 300 ducats would be necessary to complete the construction. Meanwhile, the council decided not to spend any more money on the Loggia, since the city of Vicenza had pledged itself to pay 24,000 ducats in three annual installments as its share of the expenses of the war Venice was waging against the Turks. According to ZORZI, 1965 (I), p. 112, Vicenza contributed 12,000 ducats to the war costs and equipped two triremes, *L'Uomo marino* and the *Torre di Vicenza*, respectively commanded by the two Vicentine "sopracomiti" Giacomo Trissino and Lodovico Porto. See also ZORZI, 1965 (I), doc. 13.

[22] A further request for 40 ducats for the Loggia was put forward by the *presidenti* on 26 December 1571: see MAGRINI, 1845-46, p. 166.

[23] See ZORZI, 1965 (I), p. 115 and n. 49. Despite the refusal to consider further requests for funds for the construction of the Loggia formulated by the *deputati* in the abovementioned deliberations of 23 December 1571, eighteen years later the Commune purchased the house with a shop at the corner of Contra' dei Giudei (Archivio Notarile di Vicenza, notary Carlo Cavalcabò, 30 March 1589), another house belonging to one Lodovico dall'Armi, and (in 1592) yet another house adjacent to these two (Archivio Notarile di Vicenza, notary Carlo Cavalcabò, 18 June 1592). A century after the battle of Lepanto (on 20 September 1671) the council approved the acquisition of the house adjacent to the Loggia facing onto the Piazza and also stipulated that renovations be carried out to render it suitable for the captain's residence; until this time his domestic staff had been lodged in a rented apartment. ZORZI 1965 (I), pp. 115 and 123 and doc. 22, publishes the proposal for a contract to demolish the house of Gabriele Angelico and to construct another near the Loggia. This document, which was discovered by Fasolo, enabled the author to state that in the proposed contract it was intended to add only one arch ("poggiolo sopra la piazza") to the Loggia, a decision that must have been strongly opposed by artists and by other citizens at the time and therefore was abandoned.

[24] See MAGRINI, 1845-46, p. 166; PÉE, 1941, p. 143. See also ZORZI, 1965 (I), p. 112, n. 26, referring to MAGANZA's (1571) reports of rejoicing.

[25] See MAGRINI, 1845-46, p. 166, who recalls that the motto "CIVITAS DICAVIT" appeared on the lateral façade, and under the central balcony was a brief appeal imploring that the monument endure externally as homage to the magistrate who had contributed so much to the completion of the work. See FACCIOLI, 1776-1804, I, pp. 147, 192 and passim; CASTELLINI, 1628 (1885 ed.), p. 125; see also PÉE, 1941, p. 144.

[26] See ZORZI, 1965 (I), p. 112, who records the verses in Paduan dialect celebrating Bernardo's exploits, written by the poet-cum-painter G. B. Maganza; on another of Bernardo's works, see ZORZI, 1965 (I), pp. 283-284.

[27] For an interpretation of the statues and inscriptions, see notes 51-55 below.

[28] See below, pp. 70-71.

[29] See MAGRINI, 1845-46, p. 167, who says that this information about the paintings provides an additional historical basis for dating the building, since Fasolo is known to have died on 1 September of that year (1572). It is, therefore, surprising to find MAGRINI, 1845, p. 51, placing in the year 1576, among buildings with a "secure date," the "Loggia Delegatizia" built by Palladio in the "Piazza Maggiore." Possibly this date refers to the completion of the work. On p. 21 Magrini mentions G. B. Ber-

nardo's involvement in the work and emphasizes Palladio's novelty for his time, as the chronological division into the following five periods shows: I. medieval buildings; II. buildings in the Renaissance style; III. buildings in the "modern" Palladian style; IV. buildings of the decadence (the Seicento and the first half of the Settecento); V. buildings of the "risorgimento" (from 1750 on). See also PÉE, 1941, p. 144.

[30] MAGRINI, 1845-46, pp. 166-167, reports the deliberations of the council during the session of 28 December 1582. This document (Archivio di Torre, *Libro Parti*, III, p. 407) is also published by ZORZI, 1965 (I), p. 114 and p. 121, doc. 17.

[31] MAGRINI, 1845-46, p. 167, records an order to pay 210 ducats "per satisfare gli obblighi del lavoro eseguito da M. Battista di Guglielmo" among the minutes of the council meeting held on 3 May 1586. He comments that we do not know what sort of work the artist provided, but that at the time he was working on the loggias of the Basilica. ZORZI, 1965 (I), p. 114 and p. 122, doc. 18, in reporting this document (Archivio di Torre, *Libro Parti*, III, p. 525), identifies the artist as Battista Marchesi della Porta Pusterla, a joiner and carpenter who made the seats and benches under the Loggia and who some years earlier had contracted to make several of the arcades of the Basilica loggias, but did not fulfill his contract.

[32] See CASTELLINI, 1628, passim, who wrote that "è opera dell'eccellente architetto Andrea Palladio" and regretted that "è opera superbissima ma non perfetta" (i. e., not completed). See also PÉE, 1941, p. 144.

[33] See MAGRINI, 1845-46, p. 167. ZORZI, 1965 (I), p. 111; ZORZI, 1909, had already pointed out that the capital letter "I" stands for "inventor," and not for "Andrea Palladio I" who was an entirely different architect, as one absurd interpretation has it.

[34] See FASOLO, 1938, pp. 261 ff.; ZORZI, 1965 (I), pp. 111-112, nn. 17-18. Zorzi adds that Palladio was in Vicenza only on 21 April 1572, when the Loggia was already roofed, according to the lists of payments for supervision of the work on the loggias of the Basilica. Concerning Palladio's longer stay in Venice in 1571 in order to work on San Giorgio Maggiore, see CICOGNA, 1826-34, pp. 331 ff., who records an agreement in this regard between Palladio, the *capomastro* Andrea della Vecchia, and the "taiapietra" Bortolo, dated 1 August 1571.

[35] MUTTONI, 1740 (II), position 323; for the metric scale, see the frontispiece and second figure ("Piazza delli Signori") in which the finished part of the Loggia is represented (pen and wash drawing, 21.8 × 33.5 cm.). PANE, 1961 (I), p. 47 and n. 11 correctly emphasizes the unreliability of the illustrations accompanying the anonymous work by the same author entitled *Architettura di Andrea Palladio di nuovo ristampata... con le osservazioni dell'Architetto N. N. e con la traduzione francese* (Venice, 1740). Bertotti had already made the same observation. See also FRANCO, 1962 (I), pp. 147-155. Among the leading architects of eighteenth-century Vicenza, Francesco Muttoni is usually considered to be a Baroque reelaborator of Palladio's architecture and the initiatior of a proto-neoclassical revival of Palladian themes which was to continue throughout the next century. A somewhat neglected personality, he is discussed by TAFURI, 1965, pp. 832-841, who says that the attitude of freedom and openmindedness characteristic of Palladio (a means of overcoming the contradictions inherent in mannerism) recurs to some extent in Muttoni, but more as intuition than as the fruit of profound meditation, susceptible to a wide range of suggestions that can be fused or juxtaposed. In this sense the 1740 edition of Palladio's treatise, which Muttoni edited, is extremely significant in the contrast between the purity of the orders and structures and the heavy baroque frames surrounding them. On Muttoni, see also BRENZONI, 1931, p. 300.

[36] Cf. the well-known work in five volumes by LEONI, 1715, and LEONI, 1721. See also WITTKOWER, 1954, pp. 310-316.

[37] BURLINGTON, 1730. On Burlington's work, see PANE, 1961 (I), p. 46 and passim.

[38] PÉE, 1941, pp. 144-145, notes that the building hasn't undergone further changes; its aspect today corresponds with that of 1572. Only the interior decoration is now lacking. All the council's documents indicate that the Loggia was built in a

ANDREA PALLADIO ARCHITETTO

David Roffi del: e Scol:

XII - Ottavio Bertotti Scamozzi, *Side elevation of the Loggia del Capitaniato.*
From *Le fabbriche e i disegni di Andrea Palladio...*, Vicenza, 1776, I, pl. XV

very short time, having been begun and finished in less than year. This circumstance and the not inconsiderable sum of 1,640 ducats allotted for the purpose seem to prove that the building was not reconstructed from its foundations but that at least the outer walls of the old Loggia were utilised. This hypothesis is confirmed by the observation that the council in 1565 had approved the purchase of adjacent houses as far as the corner of the Contra' dei Giudei in order to extend the building in that direction. Although there is no proof that this was ever done, and although the three private residences were acquired much later (in 1582, 1672, and in the nineteenth century), the state of the construction (with scarfs on the side walls and with a sudden break in the cornice) and all the reminders of the old Loggia show that it is unfinished as it stands, with only three bays. The city council on 23 December 1571 referred to "quella parte, che è principiata." If the building had been entirely demolished, new foundations would have been laid for the whole structure and not only for a part of it. It is therefore clear that the alternatives placed before the Council—i. e., restoration or a new building—must have been resolved by a compromise. The new Loggia assumed an entirely different aspect, although the main walls were preserved. Pée's conclusion is that Palladio was restricted by a preexisting structure and was therefore unable to carry out his project as he would have wanted to. By this argument the author takes over BORTOLAN's suggestion (1892, passim) that Palladio preserved the old plan with its distribution of spaces but framed the façades in his own classical lines, and perhaps his being bound by preexisting levels and apertures explains the "licences" he took, for which he was criticised by others.

[39] PÉE, 1941, see note above. See also MAGRINI, 1845-46, pp. 170-171, who writes that the council's deliberation of 1565 surely proposed a building extending from the corner of the old Loggia at the end of the neighboring street to the Contra' dei Giudei; but the acquisition of the three houses in between was never effected. An examination of the lists of property belonging to the commune of Vicenza shows that only in 1582 did it purchase the corner house and then only because the owner, Cecilio Cadamosto, offered it; in 1671 the commune acquired the one adjacent to the Loggia, which belonged to Gabriele Angeli, so that the Venetian captain would have better living quarters for his family; the third house, in the middle, remained private property. Therefore when the new Loggia was approved in 1571, the city meant to "riparar le rovine della vecchia" without enlarging it. Nevertheless, the original proposal was not forgotten and possibly a passage in the council's deliberations of 23 December allotting new sums but stating that no further requests were to be made "quanto però a quella parte che è principiata" alludes to it. Posterity was left to believe that the desire to construct a new Loggia more suited to the dignity of the great citizens' councils had not been abandoned: possibly the work was interrupted for the same reason (shortage of funds) that held up work on the Basilica. The scarfs that were left in place when building operations were broken off show that the artist had a larger plan in mind.

[40] On the Basilica, the project for San Petronio, and the restoration of the Doge's Palace, see PANE, 1961 (I), pp. 143 ff., pp. 301-302, and p. 36 respectively. See also PANE, 1961 (II), pp. 119 ff.

[41] In fact, there is no staircase in the Loggia that connects the two floors: the upper hall is accessible through the older building in the rear, once the property of the Verlato family. Concerning the Palazzo Trissino-Baston, designed by Vincenzo Scamozzi in 1592 for Count Galeazzo Trissino and now the Town Hall, see BARBIERI, CEVESE, MAGAGNATO, 1956, pp. 94-95 (pp. 81 ff.).

[42] BERTOTTI SCAMOZZI, 1776-83 (I); the best-known edition is that of G. B. Rossi of 1786. The work was also published in French; see BERTOTTI SCAMOZZI, 1776-83 (II). Cf. also BERTOTTI SCAMOZZI, 1785 and 1797. On Bertotti's work, see n. 117 below.

[43] See PANE, 1961 (I), pp. 357-358.

[44] See PANE, 1961 (I), pp. 357-358. CEVESE, 1962, pp. 287 ff., n. 14, has recently pointed out that the face of the brick shaft appears to have been carried straight up flush with the limestone base, instead of having been set back about two centimeters to allow for the stucco facing (as in the portico of Palazzo Chiericati

or in the interior of Palazzo Valmarana). He suggests that the columns of the Loggia were not covered in marble stucco but in exposed brick, and that the rust-red color of the brick contrasted with the colors of the stone and the stucco bas-reliefs, thus lending the building a pictorial quality rich in warm tones. PANE, 1964, pp. 120-121, in reply, has rightly observed that the limestone blocks of the bases do not stop at the cavetto but are carried on into the shafts. That this irregularity in execution, which stands out even more clearly when seen in relation to the corners of the building, would have been intended as part of the finished effect is out of the question. Pane also points out that the stone socle is lower on the side than in the front by a depth of about three bricks, while the cavetto of the side columns is much higher than that of the front columns. All this aside, Pane notes that we cannot credit Palladio with intending to produce a chromatic effect consisting of an alternation between red bricks and white interstices, for the bas-reliefs with the trophies were also white, as is proven by the few fragments remaining. The use of brick in the façade of the cloister of the Convento della Carità in Venice assumes a different significance, as there the brickwork is the dominating and essential element, and the part constructed in stone is limited only to those features which structurally had to be of that material. The reference in the Venetian building to Bramante's Belvedere in the Vatican is explicit. In the Vicentine Loggia, however, the columns must have been covered with a thin layer of stucco smoothed over at the base so as to fuse with the limestone surface. The problem has been briefly examined by PÉE, 1941, p. 150, who notes that today the bricks are exposed on the half-columns and on those parts of the wall where the ornament has crumbled away. Since there is almost no trace of a layer of plaster, one cannot say for sure whether the Loggia was entirely covered with stucco, but it is highly probable. Pée adds that the stucco ornament bears no traces that might lead us to think it was painted. CEVESE, 1965, pp. 308-310, repeats his arguments with numerous detailed observations, comparing the perfect workmanship of the columns of the Loggia del Capitaniato to the careless execution of those of Palazzo Chiericati, the Malcontenta, and Palazzo Valmarana, where the stucco was removed during restoration. The idea that the bricks were left uncovered had already been suggested by NEGRIN, 1881, p. 23 and passim, and again by DE MORI, 1932, pp. 19-21, who wrote in his study of the Loggia that Palladio succeeded extremely well in fusing the uncovered brickwork of the medieval structure with the imposing composite order of his unfinished portico. This theory is repeated by ZORZI, 1965 (I), p. 117, who maintains that the building exploits pictorial effects through the varying colors of the materials employed. The shafts of the columns, consisting of uncovered bricks, give the two façades a warm tone, broken only by a few lighter or darker stones (the bases and capitals of the columns and the brackets). See also ACKERMAN, 1966, p. 123, who states that the brick surface of the columns was not meant to be covered with stucco, as Loukomski has pointed out (see n. 162); Ackerman interprets this chromatic effect as a sign of "the unclassical spirit of Palladio's last years," consistent with the windows cutting through the architrave and the triglyph-supports of the balconies.

[45] PANE, 1961 (I), p. 358.

[46] PANE, 1961 (I), p. 358; on Hellenistic architecture, see also CREMA, 1959, p. 550, fig. 724 (the Arch of Septimius Severus) and pp. 215 ff., figs. 211-213 (the arch in Orange). Palladio also made a study of the Arch of the Gavii in Verona, and when the latter was reconstructed in 1932 (after its demolition in 1805) his four drawings made between 1530 and 1540 (now in the Biblioteca Comunale in Verona) were used, along with the many drawings by Antonio and G. B. Sangallo, Serlio, Falconetto, Sanmicheli, and other Renaissance architects (cf. ANTI, 1921-22, pp. 121-138).

[47] "Le grandi Colonne, come vedrassi ne' Disegni, hanno 10. diametri e ⅓ d'altezza, hanno Composito il Capitello, ed Attica la base, cioè quella che il Palladio ne' suoi precetti prescrive per l'Ordine Corintio; la trabeazione è circa la quinta parte della Colonna; e gli Archi, che sono alle Colonne frapposti, hanno d'altezza due larghezze e la quinta parte; le proporzioni delle altre parti vedonsi nella tavola XIV". BERTOTTI SCAMOZZI, 1776-83 (I), I, p. 45.

[48] BERTOTTI SCAMOZZI, 1776-83 (I), I, pp. 45 ff. writes: "Dietro a tali premesse si renderà più facile l'intendere i Disegni di questa Fabbrica; circa la quale mi resta solo ad enunciare un madornale difetto ch'ella contiene, il quale non si può certamente ascrivere che ad un'arbitraria e poco accurata esecuzione. L'errore ch'io accenno, e che disgusta anche i meno intendenti d'Architettura, riscontrasi nell'architrave dell'Ordine Composito principale, il quale resta interamente tagliato dalle finestre del Piano superiore. Egli è un errore, come ognun vede, di molto peso, e diformante la venustà di questo prospetto; né certamente può essere nato d'altronde che dalla inemendabile audacia degli esecutori, o dalla loro imperizia; essendo forse in quel tempo il Palladio dalla sua Patria lontano, o essendo accaduta una tal esecuzione, come pensano alcuni, dopo la di lui morte." According to Bertotti Scamozzi, the fact that Palladio's name appears on the architrave at the side proves that he had died before the building was finished: "Ch'egli mancato fosse di vita pria dell'esecuzione di questa Fabbrica, serve per dimostrarlo la sola iscrizion del suo nome incisa nella Cornice architravata. Queste onorate memorie diringonsi unicamente all'utile fine di risvegliare negli uomini un forte amor per la gloria, e per impegnare la penetrazione de' loro ingegni in lunghi e penosi studj, e per animargli alle grandi imprese colla lusinga d'immortalare il loro nome; ma questa troppo tarda e miserabile ricompensa dalle onorate fatiche dei dotti suol essere dagli autori viventi modestamente negletta. E come potria supporsi, che il Palladio permesso avesse in questo caso la incisione del suo nome, se negligentato egli aveva un tal fregio nelle sue Opere più cospicue, e massimamente nell'insigne Basilica, che pur seppe eccitargli nell'animo, come altrove diremo, una vivissima compiacenza?" PANE, 1964, p. 121, refers not to the supposed error of the interruption of the architraves but to other irregularities in the construction of the Loggia, especially the detail of the column bases, when he writes that these irregularities are probably to be ascribed to Palladio's absence from Vicenza and to the distress he suffered following the death of his two sons in 1572, the decisive year for the erection of the part of the building still standing. See below, note 202.

[49] LAMPERTICO, 1880, p. 26, affirms that although Palladio conformed to precepts derived from his study of the antique, he had a marvelous way of adapting his buildings to existing circumstances and took advantage even of the difficulties which sites presented. This idea has occasionally been suggested in the past because of the freedom with which Palladio used the classical orders, even in irregular topographical situations which were not very well adapted to the application of the canons (note Palladio's "inventioni per diversi siti" in the Quattro Libri, Bk. II, pp. 71-73); the concept has been extended to cover the whole of Palladio's work as a means of acknowledging his rare gift for town-planning. In fact, it appears to be a fundamental element in his oeuvre: he did not imagine his buildings—as many neoclassical architects did—as alien to their urban surroundings, but on the contrary saw them as a part of everyday reality. This is true of all his works, from Palazzo Chiericati to Palazzo Valmarana, including the villas, the Venetian churches, and the Loggia del Capitaniato. On Palladio's conception of town-planning, see BETTINI, 1961 (II), pp. 9-11 (see also note 186 below). Cf. also PANE, 1962, pp. 22 ff., and ZOCCA, 1960, pp. 69 ff. LOTZ, 1966, pp. 124-126, does not admit Palladio's vocation as a town-planner; he denies that the Loggia can be understood as an attempt on Palladio's part to resolve urban problems and adds that the idea of the giant order on the façade renders it autonomous in comparison with preexisting structures; but these extrinsic remarks do little to illuminate the far more complex question of Palladio's personality as an architect. See ZORZI, 1967, pp. 168 ff., p. 171.

[50] The Serliana may also be found in the rear façade of the Villa Godi at Lonedo. It is the keynote of the composition of the Basilica's double loggia, and Palladio adopted it at the Villa Barbaro at Maser, at the Villa Angarano at Angarano, in his projects for San Petronio in Bologna, and so forth. Concerning the proportions of the side façade, see BERTOTTI SCAMOZZI, 1776-83 (I), I, p. 45, who points out that the height of the columns is equal to 10¼ times the diameter, and the cornice is a little less than one-eleventh the height of the column (Figs. XIV-XV). Note, however, that the use of the Serliana in the Basilica is completely new, as it is developed in depth with the supports doubled (see PANE, 1961 (I), p. 146).

[51] For the inscriptions, see FACCIOLI, 1776-1804, p. 192; PÉE, 1941, pp. 148 ff.; ZORZI, 1965 (I), p. 113, n. 29.

[52] BORTOLAN and LAMPERTICO, 1880, p. 218, suggest that the two inscriptions should be completed in the following manner: [PUBLICA RES CHRISTI] BELLI SECURA QUIESCO (under Victory); and [NAUPACTI POSTQUAM] PALMAM GENUERE CARINAE (under Peace).

[53] WITTKOWER, 1962, p. 87, n. 2.

[54] See PÉE, 1941, p. 150 and n. 7, who quotes the opinion of Prof. Knoche of Göttingen on this question.

[55] RIPA, 1603, p. 203, and 1764-67; WITTKOWER, 1962, p. 87, n. 2.

[56] See ZORZI, 1951, pp. 141-157, especially pp. 152-153. See also MAGAGNATO, 1952, pp. 22-23 and fig. 30, who emphasizes the way in which the style of decorators and stuccoworkers was adopted by the Rubini even in stonecarving; he also says that the statues of the Loggia and the Rotonda express "a willing acceptance of Vittoria's ideals of plastic synthesis and broad picturesque effects."

[57] "Nell'estremità dei piedistili che fanno poggio alle scale delle logge vi sono statue di Messer Lorenzo Vicentino scultore molto eccellente" (PALLADIO, 1570, p. 18). These examples of Rubini's work led VENTURI, 1938, p. 326, to give a somewhat unfavorable judgment of his ability, calling him a very mediocre follower of Vittoria, although admitting that his statues have a certain value (certainly because of Palladio's sketches) when considered in relation to the architecture. ZORZI, 1951, pp. 141-157, esp. p. 148, observes that even considering the present condition of the statues, which have eroded over the years, they must be termed youthful works since they really do not seem to have been carved by a " scultore molto eccellente," which Rubini certainly was by 1570 when Palladio published his treatise.

[58] Lorenzo Rubini, together with the painter Giovanni Antonio Fasolo, worked on the decoration of the wooden theatre set up by Palladio in 1561 for the Academy in the hall of the Basilica (to be used for the presentation of Piccolomini's Amor costante), and also on the decoration for Trissino's Sofonisba —played in the same theatre, which had been adapted for the purpose—the following year. See ZORZI, 1951, pp. 141-157, esp. p. 147 and n. 2, where he publishes the results of his researches in the Archivio Notarile and in the Biblioteca Civica of Vicenza. Although Lorenzo Rubini was inscribed as a member of the masons' and sculptors' guild in Vicenza in 1549, when he was working under maestro Giovanni da Pedemuro (nicknamed after the street on which he lived), he cannot be considered one of the latter's pupils, because Giovanni died in 1550 and at his death his workshop ceased to function, since his sons died young and his associate, Girolamo Pittoni, left Vicenza. On Giovanni da Pedemuro, see ZORZI, 1937, pp. 96 ff.

On Giovanni da Pedemuro as Palladio's master, see ZORZI, 1922, pp. 120-150; ZORZI, 1949, pp. 140-152.

[59] See PREDELLI, 1908, pp. 176-178, who, referring to the caryatid on the right (June 1553), informs us that a certain Master Giovanni worked on it for seven days and a "maestro Iacomo taglialapietra" for another five, and for an additional sixty-five days following, a "maestro Lorenzo vicentino intagliatore." Work on the caryatid on the left, which was begun by Giovanni da Sasso and finished by a stonecarver named Giannantonio Vicentino and his assistant, lasted sixty-eight days, beginning 6 September 1554. ZORZI, 1951, p. 149, observed that the two sculptures differ extremely in quality, and that Vittoria carved his own initials only on the one at the right, to show that he fully approved of Rubini's work.

[60] See ZORZI, 1951, pp. 149 ff. In 1549 Lorenzo was still a "garzon"; in the documents he is referred to as an "intaiador" in 1553 and two years later as a " sculptor." Having returned to Vicenza in 1556, he worked on decorations commissioned by the Accademia Olimpica and was numbered among its "conservatori," along with Palladio, who was one of its founders (1555). It is possible that the decorative group with Atlas (or Hercules?) over the main door to the salone of the Basilica may also be attributed to Rubini—together with the stuccoes of Palazzo di Montano Barbaran in Via Porti and the monument to Ippolito Porto in San Lorenzo in Vicenza—because of its close analogy

with the stuccoes of the Loggia and because of the fact that the two groups were almost certainly made during the same period (but see BARBIERI, 1970, pp. 112-114 and p. 120, nn. 95-112). For a discussion of these works and of Rubini's personality as an artist see Zorzi, who bases his information on the eighteenth-century manuscript memoirs of ZIGGIOTTI (Biblioteca Civica, Vicenza), which deal with the acts and minutes of the Academy. Rubini collaborated with other academicians (among them Giovanni Antonio Fasolo) in preparing the sets for the presentation of Terence's *Andria*, translated by the academician Alessandro Massaria (1557); he seems to have carved the statues that formed part of the set for an *apparato* with an imaginary temple attributed to Palladio, erected for the "Olympic games" in 1558. He also completed a statue of Vulcan in the stucco room of the Vicentine Academy, and he worked in terracotta, although none of his works in this medium is known to us, with the possible exception of the Atlas (?) group at the Basilica.

[61] The attribution of the Loggia stuccoes to Vigilio Rubini was made by BARBIERI-CEVESE-MAGAGNATO, 1956, p. 95 (signed F. B.). ZORZI, 1951, p. 152, had previously excluded this attribution.

[62] The stuccoes were already finished in 1575, as the following phrase demonstrates: "... il palazzo del Capitano molto bene inteso con studi con statue et altri ornamenti regi..." (SANSOVINO, 1575, p. 114).

[63] See FASOLO, 1938, passim, and ZORZI, 1951, p. 152, n. 7. Zorzi refers to Fasolo's opinion expressed in a letter of 1936 but never published. See also ZORZI, 1965 (I), p. 113; VENTURI, 1938, p. 329, proposes a decoration begun by Lorenzo Rubini and Ottaviano Ridolfi and continued by Agostino and Vigilio Rubini.

[64] See ZORZI, 1951, p. 152, who adds: "On the façade looking onto the Piazza, the half-spandrels of the loggia arches flanking the brackets supporting the dentillated cornice on which the balconies of the windows above rest are adorned with six river gods, while the spaces between the brackets themselves are filled with lavish cartouches. The nude figures of the bearded river-gods are magnificent...; their muscular arms are shown holding vases from which water gushes forth. On the other hand, large masks decorate the spaces beside the balustrades of the first-storey windows, and above them the wall is adorned with narrow panels containing trophies commemorating the victory of Lepanto... ."

[65] ZORZI, 1951, p. 152.

[66] On Palazzo Valmarana, see PANE, 1961 (I), pp. 351-353.

[67] Note the pilasters of the outermost bays before the corner turrets in the façade of Villa Trissino at Cricoli: the lower ones, which flank little arcades surmounted by oculi and in the center serve as supports for the larger arches of the main portal, are fluted, and the upper ones are smooth. In the upper zone the oculi have been eliminated, and the terminal arches, which are of the same dimensions as those below, are made to serve as niches for statues. This seems to indicate a fondness on the part of the architect for the use of fluted pilasters, which can create a greater degree of chiaroscuro where no statues are involved: this observation, however, is only general, since the villa seems to be a kind of academic exercise on the Raphaelesque themes at Villa Madama, attributable to the humanist whose name it still bears and not to Palladio; cf. PANE, 1961 (I), pp. 99-100 and fig. I, p. 117. BERTOTTI SCAMOZZI, 1776-83 (I), II, pp. 48-49, pls. XXXVIII-XXXIX, does not show flutes on the pilasters of the lower storey. On the so-called Casa Cogollo, used as a notary's studio and attributed to Palladio by PANE, 1961 (I), pp. 353-354, the two fluted pilasters of the upper order were employed as a frame for a lost fresco by Fasolo, symbolic in character, which originally adorned the center of the windowless façade. As Pane has shrewdly remarked, the fluted pilasters, so uncommon in Palladio's work, take on the precious character suitable to frames like those of some Cinquecento altarpieces.

[68] On Palazzo Thiene Bonin and the problem of its attribution, see PANE, 1961 (I), pp. 359 ff., pp. 381 ff.

[69] At first ZORZI, 1951, p. 152, excluded the attribution to Rubini of the statues of the east front (the side) of the Loggia; but later (see ZORZI, 1965 [II], pp. 83-94, esp. p. 87), after a more

careful examination, he agreed that the figures of Peace and Victory might possibly be attributed to Rubini but suggested that rather mediocre assistants must have collaborated on the four figures on the upper storey. See also ZORZI, 1965 (I), p. 113.

[70] See ACKERMAN, 1966, p. 124, who says, "Excessive detail and loss of bold scale also weaken the stuccoes of the Loggia del Capitaniato," and adds, regarding the Palazzo Valmarana, that " the iconography escaped Palladio's control, too."

[71] See WITTKOWER, 1962, p. 88: "Documents show that the Loggia was built by the Community of Vicenza with extraordinary speed. On April 18th, 1571, building had not yet begun, but during the summer the structure rose quickly, and by the end of the year it was roofed in. The victory of Lepanto was won on October 7th. On the 18th of this month it became known at Vicenza, which, being Venetian territory, was particularly stirred by the great news. Its reverberations made themselves felt immediately in the decision of the overjoyed community, taken on October 26th, to contribute 24,000 ducats to the expenses of the campaign. Impressed by this feat of arms, Palladio must have changed his original plans for the Loggia, for it is evident that he could not have decided on the triumphal decorations of the main front before the middle of October. Nor does it seem probable that the triumphal arch motif of the side was introduced before Lepanto supplied a reason for it."

[72] WITTKOWER, 1962, pp. 87-88.

[73] ACKERMAN, 1966, pp. 84, 112, 122.

[74] PANE, 1961 (I), p. 60. See also PANE, 1956, p. 410.

[75] WITTKOWER, 1962, p. 87.

[76] WITTKOWER, 1962, p. 88 and p. 88, n. 2. The painting is in the Sala delle Quattro Porte in the Doge's Palace. The event is recorded by DE NOLHAC and SOLERTI, 1890, pp. 33-36, p. 98. See MOLMENTI, 1880, II, p. 103. On the taste for decorations for triumphal entries and funeral ceremonies in the Cinquecento, see CHASTEL, 1958, pp. 105 ff.

[77] See also CHASTEL, 1958, p. 87, who adds that, bearing in mind the honorary trappings, we can say that Palladio thought he had found a satisfactory solution when he combined the loggia and the triumphal arch in a permanent structure. Concerning the *sedili* in Naples and southern Italy, see VENDITTI, 1967, pp. 651, 691 ff. (the *sedili* destroyed in Naples, the Dominova in Sorrento, the *sedile* of S. Luigi in Aversa, and that of S. Oronzo in Lecce, etc., are mentioned).

[78] PUPPI, 1963, pp. 44 ff., p. 48, pp. 51-52, and passim; PANE, 1961 (I), pp. 362 ff.

[79] CHASTEL, 1960, pp. 29-33. See also PUPPI, 1963, pp. 42-43.

[80] See Borghini's sketch with the arch erected at the Canto della Paglia during the celebrations of 1565 in Florence; cf. PUPPI, 1963, p. 43.

[81] See PALLADIO, 1570, Bk. II, p. 52.

[82] The irregularities in the two windowless side rooms with flat ceilings are due to the preexisting structures. The one on the right backs onto Via Monte di Pietà and corresponds on the exterior with the remains of the Torre Verlata: a false door with an architrave is set in the side looking onto the street; the room opposite (on the left) has a blind window.

[83] The attribution was made by BARBIERI in BARBIERI-CEVESE-MAGAGNATO, 1956, p. 95. Two steps lead up to the door in the terminal apse, whereas if the pavement of the portico were to be lowered there would be three. This alteration has been suggested in view of the fact that outside the Loggia there are three steps, and inside there are only two. Regarding the outside steps, while the Basilica has recently acquired two more (uncovered when the Piazza was paved and restored in order to give the building its original appearance), the Loggia has had only one added, on account of the transversal slope in the level of the Piazza. However this may be, the section of the steps of the Loggia shows that they were not restored during the eighteenth century. That the difference in level did not exist originally is shown by the fact that the plinth below the bases of the half-columns in the interior is buried in the present pavement of Piovene stone, whereas it must originally have been visible; if it were restored, the plinth would lie flush with the point of juncture of the bases of the giant half-columns on the façade.

XIII - Ottavio Bertotti Scamozzi, *Details and transverse section of the Loggia del Capitaniato.*
From *Le fabbriche e i disegni di Andrea Palladio...*, Vicenza, 1776, I, pl. XVI

This hypothesis has been suggested by Cevese, 1965, pp. 305-315, esp. p. 310, fig. 93. As far as the actual state of the interior portico of the Loggia is concerned, the impression of strict regularity of the original structure has been spoilt by the horrible nineteenth-century mustard-colored plaster which has entirely replaced the ideal neutral white stone typical of Palladian interiors. The marble slabs at the sides of the two doors, with the names of "Vicentini caduti per la libertà d'Italia (1943-1945)" carved on them, is another violation of the original harmony.

84 See Palladio, 1570, Bk. I, pp. 60 ff. ("Delle scale e delle varie maniere di quelle"); Bk. II, p. 30 (plan of the Convento della Carità). Among the Palladian structures in which stairs are given somewhat greater importance are the Palazzo Della Torre in Verona and the " Inventione per un sito in Venezia," Bk. II, p. 72. See also Chastel, 1965, pp. 11-22.

85 See Zorzi, 1965 (I), pp. 90 ff., figs. 74-75. He agrees that the arrangement of this entire part of the Loggia is not neoclassical and points out the difference between these half-columns and those of the main staircase, copied after the shafts of the Basilica. In addition, there are no quarter-pilasters at the corners of the neoclassical staircase, but only narrow listels.

86 Since the original frescoes have disappeared, the walls of the hall of the Loggia are now decorated with paintings in the style of Zelotti, taken from the Villa Porto at Torri di Quartesolo. See Barbieri, in Barbieri-Cevese-Magagnato, 1956, p. 95. The upper hall of the Loggia was restored only a few years ago by the city of Vicenza; see Guiotto, 1964, p. 86, who lists the work undertaken (interior repairs included replacing bricks, restoring fittings and windowpanes, plastering, cleaning the wooden coffered ceiling, and reinserting Fasolo's paintings; repairs to the exterior involved renovation of the plaster and cleaning and fixing the stucco ornaments).

87 See Muttoni, 1740 (II), caption to fig. 2; Muttoni, 1740 (I), vol. IX. See also Zorzi, 1956 (I), p. 114. Regarding volume IX of Muttoni's *Architettura di A. Palladio*, published posthumously (1760)—also known with the title-page reading *Fabbriche inedite di A. Palladio in Padova, Piazzola sul Brenta e Vicenza*—see Lorenzoni, 1963, n. 1, pp. 14-21; n. 2, pp. 9-12.

88 On the Palazzo di Iseppo da Porta, see Pane, 1961 (I), pp. 159 ff., figs. 1-5, pp. 169 ff.; for Palazzo Valmarana, pp. 351 ff., figs. 1-5, pp. 367 ff.; for Palazzo Thiene Bonin, pp. 359 ff., figs. 30-34, pp. 381 ff. The palace Palladio called an "Inventione per un sito piramidale" also has seven bays with superimposed orders and three storeys; see Pane, 1961 (I), p. 277, figs. 1-3. Only in the palace he designed for Giacomo Angarano (p. 280) did the architect plan nine bays, adopting a giant order carried up over two storeys with an attic above, crowning the rectilinear entablature.

89 We quote Bertotti Scamozzi, 1776-83 (I), I, p. 44, justifying his proposal of a graphic reconstruction, albeit with due caution: "Sarebbe azzardoso il voler definire quanta estensione, qual forma, qual distribuzione di parti interne aver dovrebbe quest'Opera, allorché condotta fosse al suo termine secondo l'idea dall'Inventor concepita; imperciocché mancando non solamente il Disegno, ma ancora ogni autentico monumento alla medesima appartenente, tutto ciò che se ne potesse dire appoggiato sarebbe su deboli fondamenti. Vero è per altro, che le *morse*, le quali si osservano ne' sopraornati del Prospetto principale, ed altri segni che veggonsi nella Loggia terrena, certificano bastantemente che la lunghezza di questo Palagio doveva esser più estesa. Dietro le tracce di questo non equivoco indizio, esaminando a dovere tutte le circostanze del pezzo già edificato, mi riuscì agevole di limitarne l'estensione in maniera che corrispondendo la lunghezza all'altezza e all'area del terreno che si potrebbe occupare e alla grandiosità della Piazza, ed in fine alla magnificenza della Basilica che trovasi di riscontro, non mi sembra riprensibile la lusinga d'avere, ciò facendo, incontrata la verità del Disegno. Aggiunsi ai tre intercolumnj, che presentemente esistono, altri

quattro, facendo continuare lo stesso ordine d'ornamenti. In ciò che spetta all'interno di questa Fabbrica, e alla distribuzione delle sue parti, per l'efficaci ragioni già dette, non ho voluto in menoma guisa por mano, sembrandomi sommamente difficile l'indovinar l'intenzione dell'Architetto. Per tal ragione ho disegnato il piano della Loggia terrena, omettendo a bella posta la distribuzione de' luoghi nel piano superiore." See below, note 162.

[90] Unless other rooms are imagined corresponding with the unexecuted bays, apart from those already existing. This hypothesis may be strengthened by a document referring to the Loggia, datable around 1675 and published by FASOLO, 1938, pp. 331 ff. It gives the items of a series of works "per l'aggiunta del palazzo dell'Illustrissimo et Eccellentissimo Signor Capitanio iuxta il modello di Palladio." Item 3 states: " Il muro che si disporrà sotto la loggia non vi andrà più dovendo essere slongata detta copia quanto importa la casa che si disfà, et portate le armi che sono affine nel detto muro o stuccate, riportate in capo la loggia nelli siti medesimi che sono nel muro che confina con li Signori Scola e ridurre esse armi con il abbellimenti di stucco o pitture nello stato primiero come si trovano al presente, come anco il banco portato in capo la loggia intesta, mettendolo da parte, acciò non venghi nel disfare il muro rovinato." This information is mentioned by GIOVANNONI, 1939, n. 1, pp. 21-26, who adds that the document may be dated about 1675, but the model to which almost all the items refer must have been Palladio's.

[91] Pane accepted Bertotti Scamozzi's interpretation in the first edition of his monograph (PANE, 1949, p. 85), but revised his opinion in its second edition (PANE, 1961 [I], p. 357); he commented that if four other bays were added to those already standing, the building—deceptively containing only two interior spaces, the porticoed loggia and the large hall—would have consisted of seven bays, equal to the usual measurements of a large palace. Its representative function, both internal and external, seems to have met more adequately by only five bays. See below, notes 88, 139, 164.

[92] See PANE, 1961 (I), p. 357, n. 14; CEVESE, 1965, p. 340.

[93] See ZORZI, 1965 (I), p. 116. But even the solution with seven bays would have been justified by the urban setting, since the building would then have reached almost to the end of the side street (Contra' Cavour), entering along the edge to the Piazza dei Signori, according to an alignment which Palladio might have taken into consideration when drawing up his plan. CEVESE, 1964, p. 340, has excluded any resemblance between the Loggia in Vicenza and the Loggia Cornaro in Padua, but he does not seem convinced by the five-bay arrangement and accepts Bertotti's proposals. ZORZI, 1967, p. 171, maintains that Palladio planned the Loggia in five bays in order to align it with the northern end of the Basilica's loggias. ACKERMAN, 1966, p. 120, also favors the five bays: " The seven-bay elevation proposed by Bertotti and other early critics is oversized and counter to the tradition of civic loggias."

[94] PÉE, 1941, p. 146; ZORZI, 1965 (I), p. 155, fig. 142. We maintain that the design refers to a public loggia for Venice. Pée dates the drawing to the end of the sixties.

[95] The typically Venetian feature of masks at the arches' keystones had already been used by Palladio with different chiaroscuro effects in the flat-bossed base of the blind lunettes in the Palazzo di Iseppo da Porto. The mask in the engraving in I Quattro Libri (Bk. II, p. 15), which refers to the cortile façade of the Palazzo Thiene (PANE, 1961 [I], p. 178, fig. 19), is nearer that on the side façade of the Loggia, but it was not executed because Palladio preferred to use smooth blocks to obtain a simpler chiaroscuro, coherent with his rejection of a frieze with stucco festoons between the capitals of the façade pilasters. The motif of the smooth blocks linked to a horizontal fascia reappears in the façade of Villa Saraceno at Finale. Palladio used the head alone, without a block behind it, in the arch of Casa Cogollo nd in the portal of Palazzo Barbarano in Vicenza. Among other buildings with this motif are Sansovino's Loggetta of the Campanile of St. Mark's.

[96] See LOTZ, 1967, pp. 13-23, and SEMENZATO, 1967 (II), pp. 337-341.

[97] The podium arms flanking the staircases were apparently a feature of the since-demolished Villa Muzani alla Pisa (PANE, 1961, [I], p. 138), of the Villa Trissino at Meledo (p. 203), of the Villa Muzani at Rettorgole (p. 240), of the main façade of Villa Pisani at Bagnolo (p. 241), of Villa Poiana at Poiana (p. 243), of the project for Villa Saraceno at Finale, of Villa Emo at Fanzolo (pp. 245-246), of Villa Mocenigo on the Brenta (p. 283), and of Villa Thiene at Cicogna (p. 284).

[98] ACKERMAN, 1966, p. 120.

[99] See ZORZI, 1954, p. 112, fig. 9. See also PANE, 1961 (I), p. 357, n. 14.

[100] See PANE, 1961 (I), p. 359, n. 14. ZORZI, 1965 (I), cit., p. 115, also points out Palladio's fondness for a five-bay arcade, not only in the building in question but also in the municipal loggia at Feltre and in several designs for the façades of private palaces, such as Palazzo Civena, Palazzo di Giuseppe Porto, and the central part of Palazzo Chiericati; cf. also the Loggia Cornaro in Padua by Falconetto, which Palladio certainly knew.

[101] On Viollet-le-Duc, see NAVA, 1949, pp. 59-65, 236-241; PEROGALLI, 1954, pp. 39-44 and passim; FRANCASTEL, 1959, pp. 101-103; DE FUSCO, 1962, pp. 82-91; PANE, 1964 (II), p. 72 and passim. GIOVANNONI, 1939, pp. 21-26, esp. p. 25, objects to excessive renovation after the manner of Viollet-le-Duc, but comments that the tendency toward it dies hard. He says that when his friends in Milan disapproved of the completion of the Loggia, he tried in vain to prevent an even more serious outrage which they had not noticed, namely, the completion of the Cathedral of Pavia in a similar style but on a reinforced concrete framework. On the modern theory of restoration, see PANE, 1964-65, pp. 69 ff.

[102] See NEGRIN, 1881, pp. 7-24.

[103] The history of the "completion" of the Loggia is recounted in the booklet issued by the Municipality of Vicenza, Per il completamento della Loggia del Capitanio, 1928, p. 9: the deliberation of the city council on the proposal by Giulio Tozzi, a lawyer and member of the council, to dedicate the completion of the Loggia del Capitaniato to the memory of the Vicentine war dead is dated 5 May 1926. The Council invited a board to have the project drawn up and to plan its financing. ZORZI, 1965 (I), p. 116, mentions a project for the completion of the Loggia drawn up by the architect Luigi Toniato and presented in 1926. On 11 June 1926 the Associazione fra i Cultori d'Architettura in Milan approved the following order of the day: "Having received word that the citizens and the authorities of Vicenza propose to extend Palladio's Loggia del Capitaniato in memory of the war victory, we hope that the patriotism of our neighboring city will not, even for a noble cause, do irreparable damage to this famous building, which as it stands is a world-famous masterpiece, and any addition to it would diminish its authenticity and beauty." See also GIOVANNONI, 1939, p. 22, who relates that all the Vicentines were in favor of the completion, but opposition outside the town was strong and its arguments heavy. It was rightly pointed out that there was no definite indication of the number of arcades in the original Palladian project; some said five, others—like Bertotti Scamozzi—seven. Concerning the principles of restoration, there was strong criticism of reviving the concepts of Viollet-le-Duc regarding the reconstruction of monumental works according to a hypothetical conception of their original form, replacing the real work with a fake. The number of people who wanted to respect the old form (their opinions were authoritatively expressed by the votes of the Accademia di Belle Arti in Venice) was swelled by the artists and architects represented by the Associazione fra i Cultori d'Architettura in Milan, who pleaded that if a building was to be finished it should be done along modern lines, as a free expression of contemporary thought (as almost always had happened in the past), and not as an unsatisfactory imitation of styles of the past.

[104] See the order of the day passed on 16 June 1926 by the plenary session of the representatives of the city's artistic and cultural associations and citizens interested in art and local history, and the unanimous vote of the Commissione Provinciale dei Monumenti di Vicenza of 30 June 1926. Both votes favored the "completion" and are reported in their entirety in the booklet Per il completamento della Loggia del Capitaniato, pp. 13-15.

[105] The architect Ettore Fagiuoli's project is published in this volume. See also GIOVANNONI, 1939, p. 23.

[106] See FRANCESCHINI, 1928, pp. 302-306. After having recounted the history of the building, he points out that it is unfinished and hopes that this condition will soon be remedied; he mentions Bertotti Scamozzi's seven-bay plan, but observes p. 303) that the Loggia would certainly be no less beautiful and possibly would gain in elegance and lightness if it were heightened by two additional arches, according to the project designed by the late sig. Toniato. On the whole, he favored Fagiuoli's plan (pp. 305-306).

[107] See GIOVANNONI, 1939, p. 23.

[108] GIOVANNONI, 1939, p. 24 and passim, criticizes the results of the intervention, against which he had rightly battled for the preservation of the small adjacent houses. He seizes the opportunity to reemphasize his own hostility to modern architecture, but distinguishes between what was genuinely modern, which was gaining ground throughout the democratic world and which in Italy went to make up the rationalist movement, and the squalid, pseudo-monumental architectural schemes projected by the architects of the Fascist regime and the supporters of the "stile Novecento."

[109] The anonymous little houses beside the Loggia may be seen in the illustration published in the *Album di gemme architettoniche*, Vicenza, 1847 (lithographs by Brizeghel after drawings by Marco Moro), with the following caption: " All'Egregio e distinto signore Angelo Zamburlin - Aggiunto delegatizio - Amatore delle Arti Belle - L'Editore Antonio Barbaro D. D. D." Photographs taken before 1931 show these structures, which housed the Caffè Garibaldi on the ground floor; in the photographic archives of the Centro Internazionale di Studi di Architettura "A. Palladio," see Ferrini photos nn. 169 and 367 (1930), as well as those illustrating the booklet *Per il completamento della Loggia del Capitaniato* of 1928, passim. See also the additional plates (pp. 16-17) in TRETTENERO, 1938. On the importance of the urban surroundings, see PANE, 1959, passim, and ZEVI, 1960, passim.

[110] See GIOVANNONI, 1939, p. 26. The author, who makes a critical distinction between one period and another, maintains that although any attempt to complete a medieval building is inadmissible since the builders and masons were allowed a wide margin of interpretation in following a general plan, such an effort is sometimes permissible in a type of architecture such as that of the Renaissance, in which every detail is rigorously subordinated to a unified plan provided by the architect. Although this statement appears to be valid at first sight, it is not something that can be generalized, as every case has to be examined on its own merits. It also seems to ignore the recent interpretation of art as a process which, in the field of architecture, enables us (even in the case of works that appear to be completely defined) to suppose that the architect himself might have imagined some change or variation in those parts not yet erected. The logical conclusion, now generally accepted, is that no one can take on an artistic personality from the past in order to "complete" another person's work, which is exactly what Viollet-le-Duc set out to do. All that the modern architect can do is to attempt to reconstruct the creative process of his predecessor and to "amplify" the original conception, not "complete" it; he can achieve this by integrating the original structures with those of his own period, according to the taste of his period and to his own personal inspiration. These works must have the same freedom and lack of prejudice which have distinguished the buildings of the great architects of the past from one another. We need mention only Palazzo Barberini in Rome; here Bernini endowed the structure erected by Carlo Maderno (1625) and Borromini with an extremely individual character by adding after 1629 the central façade, which stands as a formally autonomous organism (PANE, 1953, p. 24). PEROGALLI, 1954, pp. 15 ff. and passim, lists numerous associations between heterogeneous forms occurring throughout history. An example of "amplification" rather than "completion" carried out in the twentieth century is offered by the town hall of Göteborg, where Asplund added to the existing neoclassical building a block with modern articulation which respects various features suggested by the preexisting structure; see ZEVI, 1948, p. 120 and passim. ZORZI, 1965 (I), pp. 116-117 and n. 57, accepts the "completion" of the Loggia with five bays and condemns the "volte-face." He even

says that it is absolutely necessary to repair the harm done and to carry out the unanimous wishes of the citizens of Vicenza (i.e., to complete the building); as this shows, the idea dies hard!

[111] Concerning the "sistemazione" of the Loggia, PANE, 1961 (I), pp. 358-359, states that more damage was done to the building through what Goethe called "active ignorance" than by the deterioration due to age (especially the damages to the stuccoes).

[112] See PANE, 1961 (I), pp. 43 ff.; PANE, 1962, pp. 15-30; PANE, 1964 (I), pp. 119-130.

[113] DONI, 1555. He lists the writings of the "più famosi huomini" which had appeared up to that time and were known to him; among the architects, he mentions only Bramante (p. 44) for his "cinque libri di Architettura," and Palladio (p. 155), about whom we read: "Zan' Andrea Palladio. Questo honorato huomo si può dire che sia venuto al Mondo per suscitare l'architettura. Egli di essa ha scritto et disegnato, molte, e bellissime cose pertinenti, a tutte le sorti di Edifizij, le quali è grandissimo peccato che non ha stampino; e il libro non ha Titolo, ma da quello che in esso si può imparare si puote chiamare *Norma di vera Architettura*." Doni's little book appeared fifteen years before the publication of *I Quattro Libri*. See also PANE, 1961 (I), p. 45.

[114] The first edition of Vasari's book (1550) appeared nearly twenty years before the second (1568, published by Giunti). Vasari was on good terms with Palladio and preannounces the publication of his theoretical works.

[115] GUALDO, 1958-59, pp. 91-104; Zorzi, who edited the publication, emphasizes that no biography or writing of Palladio can be studied without the help of Gualdo's little book. The biography was written about 1615 and the manuscript, which has no title, was given the one suggested two centuries ago by MONTENARI, 1749, who was the first to publish it. The biographer emphasizes the "monumental" aspect of Palladio's work, "anco negli Edifizii e case private come anco in quelli di Villa," and his many references to classical architecture: "Gran memoria del suo valore lasciò [Palladio] specialmente nella città di Vicenza, gran parte de quali sono poste in dissegno nel famoso libro ch'egli compose dell'Architettura, tanto utile e comunemente abbracciato da tutto il mondo da quelli che hanno gusto di tal arte, poiché egli non si scostò mai dalle regole e misure dell'architettura buona degli Antichi Romani, e per questo è stato stampato e ristampato molte volte, acquistando sempre maggior credito e riputazione."

This interpretation is only in part acceptable; Palladio, as has been noted, tied himself down to the canons only as a theorist and did not hesitate to violate them as an architect. See PANE, 1961 (I), pp. 69 ff.

[116] TEMANZA, 1762. Temanza's biography was republished without any changes sixteen years later (TEMANZA, 1778; for the Loggia, see pp. 284-408) and was reprinted in 1966.

[117] On Bertotti's work, see BARBIERI, 1952, pp. 153-159; PANE, 1961 (I), p. 48 and n. 15; FRANCO, 1963, pp. 152 ff.

[118] See BERTOTTI SCAMOZZI, 1761. The dialogue is dedicated "al nob. signore marchese Mario Capra." The little volume is also mentioned by BOITO, 1883, p. 293.

[119] BERTOTTI SCAMOZZI, 1761, pp. 20-22 and pls. II-III (façade and side).

[120] See also MOSCA, 1779, II, pp. 17 ff.

[121] BERTOTTI SCAMOZZI, 1761, pp. 20-22.

[122] PANE, 1961 (I), p. 48, notes that the handsome engravings in the volume are in themselves an eloquent comment on the architect's works, for the sensitive reader finds in them a graphic reproduction not only of buildings which, although completed, have suffered the ravages of time, but also of those which were only begun and of the designs for "Inventioni per diversi siti" which never went beyond the project stage; Bertotti's book deserves admiration merely because it stimulates our aesthetic appreciation.

[123] See BERTOTTI SCAMOZZI, 1761: "Il celebre architetto N.N., nell'edizione da esso fatta delle opere di Palladio, pensò di migliorare i prospetti di questa fabbrica, introducendo nei disegni della medesima alcune serie alterazioni.... Nella stessa opera gli archi del prospetto principale sono disegnati larghi piedi 8 e ½,

e sono in esecuzione piedi 9 e 1 oncia. E l'attico che è alto piedi 9, è disegnato piedi 10. Minorò di un piede l'altezza delle colonne composite minori, e cangiò il loro capitello da composito in corintio. Finalmente, oltre a molte altre minute disparità, minorò il lume degli intercolunnii laterali, alterò inoltre le proporzioni dei piedistalli sostenenti le statue e fece un piede più elevata l'altezza dei poggiuoli." Cf. note 35 above.

[124] See MILIZIA, 1787, pp. 254 ff.

[125] PANE, 1961 (I), pp. 52-53. On Milizia's theoretical formulae, see VENDITTI, 1961, passim.

[126] See MILIZIA, 1787: "In Vicenza i suoi edifici sono, la Basilica ossia palazzo della ragione; edificio gotico da lui saviamente rimodernato. Il palazzo Trissino a Cricolo, il Palazzo Tieve [sic], il palazzo Valmarana, e quelli di Barbarano, di Porto, di Chiericati, di Franceschini, e la famosa Rotonda di Capra sopra un colle. Fece anche una casa per sé. È famoso il Teatro Olimpico sul gusto antico... ."

[127] See CICOGNARA, 1810, pp. 31-33 (the author was president of the Accademia Veneta di Belle Arti).

[128] CICOGNARA, 1810, p. 8, maintains that Palladio was a Vicentine by birth, an error also found in TEMANZA, 1762. PANE, 1959 (II), p. 48, has observed that one's real citizenship is that which one chooses for oneself and not that which one receives by chance. Cicognara also gives Palladio's birth-date as 1518, instead of 1508. On Palladio's place of birth, see FIOCCO, 1933 (I); ZORZI, 1922, passim (see note 58).

[129] GALEANI NAPIONE, 1818, pp. 111-126.

[130] GALEANI NAPIONE, 1818, p. 113.

[131] GALEANI NAPIONE, 1818, p. 126.

[132] See QUATREMÈRE DE QUINCY, 1830, pp. 1-28, who does not mention the Loggia. See also QUATREMÈRE DE QUINCY, 1842-44, and PANE, 1961 (I), p. 54.

[133] SCOLARI, 1837, pp. 22-23 and passim.

[134] SCOLARI, 1837, p. 145, n. 8.

[135] SCOLARI, 1837, p. 145, who points out that Palladio was burdened by family cares and in need of patronage, and that he was often obliged to bow to fashion and to tolerate the whims and adapt himself to the economic circumstances of his supporters; this is a point that architects should bear always in mind, for they should contrive to maintain their independence and to be their own masters in carrying out their works, which they transmit to posterity rather than to the client who commissioned them.

[136] MAGRINI, 1845-46, pp. 126-171. See also notes 2 and 29 above. Elsewhere MAGRINI, 1845, p. 51 and passim, shows his acceptance of current neoclassical aesthetics when, as we have already pointed out, he labels the Baroque structures of the Seicento and the first half of the Settecento "fabbriche del decadimento." His comment that the Loggia is worthy to stand in front of its majestic sister loggias, those of the Basilica, is standard (p. 21). He mentions among the features that prove that Palladio designed the Loggia (p. 168), besides the inscription bearing his name below the side balcony, the use of proportions and members typical of Palladio's work, as Bertotti Scamozzi had already pointed out. He also emphasizes the fact that the *deputati* in charge that year were Palladio's closest friends (Giuseppe Porto, Giacomo Angarano, Girolamo Ragona, Brunoro Volpe, Orazio Thiene, etc.), each of whom had commissioned buildings for themselves from the architect. In addition, one of the two *provveditori*, Giuliano Piovene (the man who had supervised the work on the Basilica the year before), had become one of Palladio's intimates through a mutual friend, Emanuele Filiberto, and appears to have commissioned a design for a house for himself " in Isola." On Magrini, see BARDELLA, 1953, pp. 5-10.

[137] See ZORZI, 1965 (I), passim.

[138] Concerning Palladio's presence in Vicenza, MAGRINI, 1845-46, p. 169, refutes the opinions of Muttoni and Bertotti Scamozzi, who held that the architect was employed in Rome during the construction of the Loggia. He affirms that Palladio was not in Rome in 1571, since his last visit there was in 1554; the notes of his expenses for the construction of Basilica show that he was in Vicenza and busily employed in building the Loggia, the construction of which was approved by the council on 18 April.

Two months earlier, on 17 February, he received 10 scudi as payment in advance on his salary for the coming months of July and August, having received 50 scudi on 22 July 1570 to cover the period until the end of the following June. After recalling that Palladio was busy at the time in Vicenza building the Palazzo Montan Barbarano, the author supposes that his need for an advance on his salary is explained by his being engaged in seeing his important publication, *I Quattro Libri*, through the press; the dedication of the book to Angarano bears the date of 1 November 1570. Magrini adds that after the payment of 17 February, Palladio received on additional 10 scudi on 13 September and another 10 on the 29th of the same month; in the period between February and September he must surely have been in Vicenza for the designing of the Loggia. On 9 October he was paid another 15 scudi to cover the period until the end of the following January. He appears therefore to have been in Vicenza in just those months when the repeated requests for funds prove that the building was being rapidly erected and had reached the stage of being roofed and adorned with the highly-approved friezes. ZORZI, 1965 (I), pp. 111 ff., n. 17, on the basis of the documents published by FASOLO, 1938, pp. 261 ff., records that Palladio was still in Venice during the months of January, February, and March of 1572 and returned to Vicenza only on 21 April of that year, when the Loggia had already been roofed. On Palladio's absence from Vicenza, see ZORZI, 1963 (I), p. 87 ff., esp. pp. 90-91.

[139] MAGRINI writes that Palladio has been reproached with a similar licence at Maser, where the arch of the central window in the upper storey likewise interrupts the entablature of the order on the façade. Some have tried to blame this defect on Monsignor Barbaro, but besides not having proof, we cannot even be sure that Palladio assisted in the construction, the date of which is uncertain (1845-46, p. 169). PANE, 1961 (I), pp. 235 ff., has also observed about the villa at Maser that the break in the horizontal cornice of the tympanum and the exceptional wealth of stuccoes recalls the pronounced pictorial quality of the Loggia. The villa is published in *I Quattro Libri*, Bk. II, p. 51.

[140] MAGRINI, 1845-46, p. 169. Cfr. also ACKERMAN, 1966, p. 122.

[141] MAGRINI, 1845-46, pp. 169 ff. Later (p. 171) the author mentions Bertotti Scamozzi's abovementioned project for the completion of the Loggia, observing that Bertotti wisely gave up any attempt to imagine further adaptations of rooms in the interior of the building which Palladio himself may never have considered, for he does not seem to have busied himself with any such schemes in the years in which the old building underwent several repairs. The drawings made by the architect Enea Arnaldi in 1786 show the building as it still stood in 1845.

[142] See BOITO, 1883, passim (see note 118). The monograph on Palladio (which appeared after the lecture; see BOITO, 1880), is divided into two parts "L'indole dell'uomo" (pp. 229-273) and "Il carattere delle opere" (pp. 275 ff.); the former is biographical, the latter critical. The Loggia del Capitaniato is not mentioned, while the temporary loggia (discussed above) accompanied by a triumphal arch, erected to celebrate Henry III's visit to Venice, is recorded on p. 306. On Boito, see GRASSI, 1959, passim.

[143] LAMPERTICO, 1880, passim.

[144] BIADEGO, 1886, passim. He discusses only the buildings Palladio erected in Verona and the neighboring countryside, where the architect stayed on several occasions in 1551, 1564, 1569, and 1570.

[145] ZANELLA, 1880, p. 73. He confirms the date (1571) and the Palladian design and mentions the preexisting loggia-type building with frescoes by Paris Bordone (1521); he also refers to the rapid erection of the new Loggia, whose coffered ceiling was embellished in 1572 with Fasolo's paintings. After having related the statues of Peace and Victory on the side façade to the battle of Lepanto, Zanella concludes that some license taken with the design (such as the architrave cut by the windows) led to a suspicion that the architect was absent or had already died when the building was erected. His name carved on the side façade and the period of construction cancel any doubt.

[146] PANE, 1961 (I), pp. 55-56.

[147] See CASTELLINI, 1885 ed., pp. 124-125 (cf. the 1628 MS,

XIV - *Elevation of the Loggia del Capitaniato with the adjacent houses before their demolition, 1930*

cited in note 25). "Palazzo del Capitanio. Si trova in mezzo alla piazza della Signoria ed è molto antico, come si può cono-scere dalle sue muraglie e dalla vecchia torre, che vi si vede appresso. Il Pagliarino dice che la comunità lo comperasse dai Verlati, e vi fabbricasse l'antica Loggia. La nuova, superbissima ma non perfetta, fu fatta sotto il reggimento del Capitano Gio-vanni Battista Bernardo, ed è opera dell'eccellente architetto An-drea Palladio, d'ordine corintio [sic] con questa dedica: Io. Bap-tistae Bernardo Praefecto civitas dicavit." The author records the verses under the central balcony: "Si quae Coelicolae magni Vicentia ponit - Vos arae et cum aris aurea templa juvant - Ingentem hanc molem alternum servata per aerum - protegite et seclis innumerabilibus - namque ipsum aeterno Bernardi struxit honori - Grati aeterna animi signa futuri sui." His note con-cludes: "La sala sopra questa loggia è adornatissima di armi e pitture di Paolo Veronese [sic], e contiene molte memorie di capitani. Nella partenza di Pietro Giustiniano gli fu dalla città nella detta sala dedicato un bel quadro di mano del Maganza, rappresentante la B. Vergine, S. Marco ed il P. Lorenzo Giusti-niani."

148 BORTOLAN and LAMPERTICO, 1880, p. 245, refer briefly to the Loggia apropos of Contra' del Monte, which until 1797 was called Contra' del Capitanio, noting that the Palace, which housed first the Venetian Captains, then the Italian prefects, then the Austrian delegates, and then the prefects of the Kingdom of Italy, in 1880 became the town hall. See also MONZA, 1888.

149 See BURCKHARDT, 1855 (1952 ed., pp. 390-391). See VEN-TURI, 1964, pp. 227-228, as well as Pfister's introduction to the Italian edition of Burckhardt's volume.

150 PANE, 1961 (I), p. 56.

151 PANE, 1961 (I), p. 86.

152 FLETCHER, 1902, p. 52. After listing the various names given to the Vicentine Loggia (Palazzo del Capitanio or del Pre-fettizio, Loggia Bernarda, Palazzo Delegatizio, Palazzo del Consi-glio, etc.), Fletcher gives an accurate description of the building and mentions the brickwork, exposed because the stuccoes had crumbled away: "The view also shows the 'dilapidated' condition of the façade, the brickwork of the columns showing where the

plaster has fallen off." On the problem of the number of bays Palladio intended the building to have, Fletcher merely repeats Bertotti's theory; however, concerning the façade he writes: "The lower portion forms a triple arcade, and the upper storey has windows and balconies projecting forward and supported on triglyph brackets. The windows of this storey cut into the architrave of the main entablature, a 'defect' in the design which is hidden by the outside blinds." Similarly, of the side façade he writes: "The upper storey on this façade has a serious 'defect,' the architrave of the main entablature being cut into by the semicircular arch of the central window." He concludes: "All reviewers of Palladio's work refer to this 'blemish' and it certainly does interfere with the dignity and even the 'raison d'être' of this important feature. ... This building was probably erected after Palladio's death, or at any rate during his absence elsewhere, this accounting for the 'faults' abovementioned."

153 See FLETCHER, 1902, p. 52. See also WITTKOWER, 1959, pp. 65-70; WITTKOWER, 1960, pp. 82-87; SUMMERSON, 1958, pp. 205 ff.

154 ANDERSON, 1909, pp. 150-151 and pl. 61.

155 After having asserted that the Loggia " belongs to a period in Palladio's life about twenty years later, and being more distinctively Palladian, is so much the poorer art" and that "yet it is still a beautiful and interesting work, and by no means lacking in originality ... ," ANDERSON, 1909, p. 150, writes: " ... the main architrave is interrupted to admit of an arch over the central window opening. This end elevation certainly shows a decadent tendency... [and] the misuse of the triglyph as a bracket is a further sign of decline." Another misunderstanding that appears in Anderson's treatment is that concerning the " poor " materials used, for which Palladio is rather to be sympathized with than blamed: "Palladio... is perhaps on the whole more to be pitied than blamed for the use of shoddy material." This error, which had already appeared in SCOTT's famous essay (1939, p. 135; Engl. ed., *The Architecture of Human-ism*, 1st ed., 1914), is discussed by PANE, 1961 (I), p. 57.

156 In addition to signs of "decadence" in Palladio's work, ANDERSON, 1909, pp. 167-168, discussing the Baroque monument

to the ducal Valier family in the Church of SS. Giovanni e Paolo in Venice—designed by Andrea Tirali (1708), with sculptures by other masters (see LORENZETTI, 1963, pp. 343-344)—writes that "the treatment of the pedestal is peculiar, and perhaps in part suggested by the side of Palladio's Prefettizio, where figures stand between the columns in a similar way. The cornice of the pedestals also forms the impost of an arch, as at the Casa del Diavolo (Palazzo Porto Breganze) in Vicenza."

[157] See BRINCKMANN, 1919, passim

[158] See GURLITT, 1914, passim. Gurlitt's ideas on Palladio were published in Italian as a preface to VINACCIA, 1921, a work which PANE, 1961 (I), p. 56, n. 30, rightly judges "indecorosa."

[159] See PANE's observations, 1961 (I), pp. 56-57.

[160] Other mistaken and unfounded statements, reminiscent of positivist thinking, occur in the very short essay by RICCI, 1923, p. xviii and illustration on p. 232 (for example, the statement that those who called Palladio "the founder of modern architecture" must have forgotten how much any transformation in art owes to collective development and to the almost spontaneous evolution of forms). In Ricci's opinion, Palladio achieved the creation of beauty through a perfect sense of proportion, which has no need to be masked by ornament. He also states that Palladio did not derive only artistic inspiration from classical architecture, but he learned as much if not more from it about how to treat structural problems and how to organize interior spaces.

[161] LOUKOMSKI, 1927 (I), p. 61. See also LOUKOMSKI, 1927 (II), pp. 8-13.

[162] LOUKOMSKI, 1927 (I), p. 61: "La loggia del Capitanio, Salle du Conseil, bâtie d'après le décret du 25 août 1571, laisse une impression d'inachevé, tandis que son motif en fait une oeuvre complète." Loukomski also accepts Bertotti's hypothesis of the seven-bay elevation and seems inclined to think that the brickwork of the columns was intended to be left uncovered ("La maçonnerie de brique qui est nue entre les colonnes, est couverte d'ornements dans toutes les autres parties, tandis que les chapiteaux et les corniches sont en pierre"). Finally, he emphasizes the large dimensions of the upper hall, which even at that time was "tellement abîmée par des changements postérieurs qu'il ne reste aucune trace de son ancienne beauté. Des meubles et des lustres de 1850-60 en complètent l'horrible aspect."

[163] LOUKOMSKI, 1927 (I), p. 36, writes: "Son mérite redouble du fait que le style de son époque avait, depuis longtemps, perdu la pureté et la rigueur du classicisme. Et son génie sut retrouver cette pureté sans se sécher dans l'observance étroite et inintelligente des règles, son art, qui peut être rapproché de l'art de Sangallo (vers la fin du XVe siècle), suivit une ligne complètement différente du baroque dans la deuxième moitié du XVIe siècle."

[164] MELANI, 1928, p. 37. We shall spare the reader any quotations from Melani's text.

[165] CANTACUZÈNE, 1928, pp. 43 ff.

[166] CANTACUZÈNE, 1928, p. 44. After having observed how Palladio's façades form "la synthèse de toute l'architecture d'une ville," and how every detail such as a window or a door seems to be awaiting some further development, Cantacuzène affirms that often we are in doubt as to the scale upon which these details were to be executed: this kind of argumentation implies a negative judgment ("l'excès de livresque, art trop intellectuel"), and its lack of justification makes it all the more unacceptable, for the same author finds in Palladio's courtyards completely different effects of sobriety, "Roman magnificence," vigorous rhythm, etc.

[167] ARGAN, 1930, pp. 327-346.

[168] BRANDI, 1960 (I), pp. 9-13.

[169] MILIZIA also criticizes the pedestals under the columns of different heights on the same plane, the cornices over the doors and windows, and the figures on the inclined cornices of the pediments, "tutto ciò dimostra l'architetto che va a tastone" (1768, pp. 281-282). He praises Palladio (calling him the "Raphael of architecture") without understanding him, because in his opinion Palladio lacks the "continuo ragionamento" which is a prerequisite for architects.

[170] ARGAN, 1930, p. 334.

[171] See BURGER, 1909, passim.

[172] ARGAN, 1930, p. 335.

[173] See BRIZIO, 1926, pp. 213-242. Another feature that Palladio and Veronese share in common is the *di sotto in sù* view typical of the painter's works, which reappears in Palladio's buildings, meant to be seen from immediately below to produce a foreshortened effect. See BRIZIO, 1960, pp. 19-25; also PIGNATTI, 1958, pp. 200-213.

[174] ARGAN, 1956, pp. 387 ff. On Sanmicheli, see ZEVI, 1959, pp. 294-295; ZEVI, 1966 (II), col. 691 ff.

[175] PANE, 1962, p. 17, has reassessed Sanmicheli's role in Palladio's formation, contrary to ARGAN's theory (1956, p. 389) that all the Palladian palaces derive from Bramantesque sources furnished by examples like the Palazzo Caprini, which is certainly valid for the Palazzi Iseppo da Porto and Thiene. Pane points out the exceptional thematic variety Palladio introduced into the composition of the palaces.

[176] See PANE, 1962, pp. 17 ff.

[177] WILLICH, 1932, p. 163. This critic accepts Bertotti's suggested seven bays for the original plan.

[178] See GIOVANNONI, 1935 (I), pp. 117-120, with earlier bibliography. He maintains that the application of the classical elements was the principal problem resolved in the façades, and that these elements were conceived for quite another purpose than to be carried out in stucco and applied to a building of several storeys, in order to accentuate the divisions between the latter.

[179] GIOVANNONI, n. d. [1935?] (II), p. 238. See ZEVI, 1960, pp. 115-118 for the limitations of Giovannoni's interpretations.

[180] VENTURI, 1940, pp. 330 ff. On p. 477, fig. 437, Venturi publishes a Palladian design for a triumphal arch, in which he was able to find a reference to the composition of the Loggia del Capitaniato.

[181] VENTURI, 1940, p. 470. Curiously enough, the author mentions fluted columns in the façade, instead of the smooth ones which are in fact there.

[182] ARGAN, 1930, p. 333.

[183] Among the more recent Palladian studies, undertaken between 1940 and 1950, we refer the reader to those of DALLA POZZA (1941, passim, and 1943, passim). A tireless researcher, Dalla Pozza has ransacked the archives for information concerning Palladio, and PANE, 1961 (I), p. 63, mentions his original contribution to the critical understanding of numerous documents. PÉE, 1941, passim, should also be consulted for his scrupulous philological contribution to the study of Palladio's secular commissions. His essay is accompanied by lengthy discussions of the "symbolical" and "philosophical" value of Palladio's buildings and on their "significance" beyond their artistic quality, rendering this part of his work unacceptable. We shall not, of course, list the vast number of essays of a laudatory and dilettantish nature, quoting only FRANCIA (1949, p. 26 and passim) as an example of this kind of treatment, which merely repeats the standard expressions of earlier writers (GIOVIO, 1782, passim). See also FERRARI, 1961, pp. 163 ff.; FERRARI, 1965, pp. 363-391; TIMOFIEWITSCH, 1960, pp. 174-181.

[184] See PANE, 1961 (I), p. 144.

[185] See FIOCCO, 1959, pp. xi ff. On this subject, see also FIOCCO, 1949, pp. 184-187; MAGAGNATO, 1950, pp. 121-130.

[186] See BETTINI, 1961 (I), pp. 89-98, especially p. 96. The fountain, finished in 1550, is described by Girolamo Gualdo.

[187] See MICHALSKI, 1933, pp. 88-109.

[188] BECHERUCCI, 1936, pp. 53-59 and passim. Referring to Palladio's work, Becherucci states that "the classical has become a lyrical substance.... The unfinished Loggia del Capitaniato appears to be a gigantic fragment, like one of Piranesi's ruins, a somber vision sprung from the almost-tormented emotions of mannerism...." See also BECHERUCCI, 1964, cols. 443-478.

[189] PEVSNER, 1943, passim; PEVSNER, 1956, pp. 81-84.

[190] WITTKOWER, 1962, pp. 82 ff.

[191] CHASTEL, 1956, pp. 83-90; CHASTEL, 1958, pp. 111-121, p. 457.

XV - MARCO MORO, *View of the Loggia del Capitaniato and its surroundings.*
From *Album di gemme architettoniche*, Venice, 1847

[192] BETTINI, 1961 (I), pp. 96-97. According to this distinguished scholar, Palladio's work may be defined as mannerist for weightier reasons than the obvious congruence with definitions, but his type of mannerism is related to the Veneto and is different from that of central Italy. In Bettini's opinion, the Florentine Renaissance was steeped in the "idea" of space and the Venetian in the "experience" of it, hence the use of geometric perspective and plastic design in the former, and of aerial perspective and tonal gradations in the latter. The mannerist crisis was brought about in both cases by the discredit into which representation as a law in itself had fallen, a characteristic evident in the philological changes (the relationship between design and the idea of space in the Tuscans, between color and experience of the world in the Venetians). See also BETTINI, 1949, p. 55.

[193] See PALLUCCHINI, 1959, pp. 38 ff. Giulio Romano's influence on Palladio is supported by GOMBRICH, 1934, pp. 79 ff. and 1935, pp. 79 ff., 121 ff., and is taken up by TAFURI, 1966, pp. 54 (n.), 81.

[194] See TAFURI, 1966, p. 22 and passim (on Palladio, pp. 46, 76 ff., 80-93). The author extends the generally accepted meaning of Mannerism and sees in the ambiguous tension created between vacuous elegance and tragic heresy the extension of the humanistic concept of rationality to complex structures of pluralistic significance. He insists upon the concepts of "research" and of "experiment" because they are typical of the Mannerist current, explaining by these the unprejudiced use of classical definitions, of multiple perspectives, and of continuous narrative typical of the leading Cinquecento artists. Tafuri also includes Michelangelo among the mannerists (p. 55).

[195] See BRANDI, 1960 (II), pp. 79 ff.; in the chapter titled "La sigla del Manierismo" he denies the legitimacy of including a great deal of the Venetian Cinquecento under this heading, formulating a negative evaluation of the phenomenon of Mannerism. He holds that it is absurd to apply such a definition to Palladio (p. 182). Here he agrees with FORSSMAN, 1965 (cf. the review by BARBIERI, 1964 (II), pp. 323-333). Among the fundamental studies of Mannerism, we refer the reader to ARGAN, 1942, pp. 181 ff., and NICCO FASOLA, 1950, pp. 175-180. Both authors emphasize the intellectual cleavage between culture and practice which is to be found in mannerist works. Nicco Fasola, whose attitude is one of ethical repulsion, partially removes the field of architecture from the definition of Mannerism, because its dedication to a real purpose always ties the work to something concrete which cannot be ignored. But this point of view seems to approach dangerously close to the anachronistic theories of architecture as an "unfreie Kunst"—already condemned by CROCE, 1946, pp. 76 ff.—since it aims at making an exception of architecture in the coordinated unfolding of the Cinquecento figurative arts. It is evident from the range of meanings given the term Mannerism that it is used with great ambiguity and with a different significance for everyone; it is used to signify everything from stylistic development to historical chronology, to evaluation, historical change, a category, etc. For a résumé of these meanings, we refer the reader to NICCO FASOLA, 1950, pp. 175 ff., who concludes that Mannerism is a spiritual attitude, or a particular mode of artistic conduct. Artists believe in a preexisting form, valid in itself, to which they have to adapt their content. See LOTZ, 1961, pp. 239 ff.; WEISE, 1962, pp. 27-38.

[196] BATTISTI, 1960, p. 225 and passim.

[197] PEVSNER, 1967, p. 309 and passim.

[198] ACKERMAN, 1966, pp. 182 ff.; he states that Palladio represents " the architectural counterpart of Veronese."

[199] See ACKERMAN, 1966, pp. 124-125. WITTKOWER, 1962, p. 86, speaks of a *horror vacui* in Palladio's work; this effect, however, is more an endeavor to perfect the techniques of chiaroscuro by isolating the primary architectonic members (the columns) from the mass of the building.

[200] BLUNT, 1962, pp. 117 and 151. See also DE FUSCO, 1968, pp. 536-537, 635.

[201] See also BATTISTI, 1967, pp. 204 ff., 206. Palladio takes up his stand against Serlio, the champion of decorative Mannerism, adopting a decidedly anti-mannerist position (if by Mannerism we mean license in ornamentation and design) and condemning, among other features, the misuse of the broken tympanums and cornices springing from "cartouches" which the publisher of the *Quattro Libri* had introduced into the frontispiece on his own initiative. See PANE, 1961 (I), pp. 77 ff.

[202] See ZEVI, 1966 (I), cols. 60, 64, 65. Elsewhere ZEVI, 1964, pp. 21 ff., examines the three fundamental components of Mannerism (the politico-religious reaction, intellectualism, and elegant virtuosity), excluding from it the figure of Michelangelo.

[203] See LAVAGNINO, 1960, passim, who insists that Palladio's longest sojourn in Rome (from the autumn of 1545 until July of 1547) coincides with one of the most crucial moments in the artistic life of that city. The list of his contacts with mannerist circles have recently been augmented by BARBIERI, 1964 (I), pp. 49-63, who concludes that in effect Palladio's situation as a genius, as isolated as the provincial culture from which he came, becomes apparent only when, from time to time, we follow the route of his arduous creative processes.

[204] See ZEVI, 1966 (I), col. 64.

[205] ZEVI, 1966 (I), cols. 74 ff. See HAUSER, 1956, II, pp. 151 ff. and passim, for the sociological framework of Mannerism. A few notes on Palladio's Mannerism may be found elsewhere in HAUSER's writings (1965, pp. 262-263), in which he affirms that the predominant classical element in Palladio's work enables critics to ignore the mannerist substratum, or to accept it "*en bloc*"; but Hauser does not show where he is able to isolate this substratum. He has recently declared that Palladio is one of the chief exponents of the mannerist vision, if the component parts of his works and their implications are analyzed, where the dialectic contrast and reconciliation of the two stylistic principles typical of Mannerism—i. e., classicism and anti-classicism, rationalism and irrationalism—are revealed. See HAUSER, pp. 187 ff.

[206] PANE, 1961 (I), p. 71 and passim. On the last period of Palladio's activity in Vicenza, see also FRANCO, 1962 (II), pp. 202-206, who accepts Pane's interpretation of Palladio's later works—including the Loggia (p. 205)—while at the same time he recognizes in them some aspects of Mannerist culture.

[207] PANE, 1961, (I), pp. 71-72. SEMENZATO, 1967 (I), p. 351, admits that Palladio was capable of using the elements of Renaissance architecture with a liberty, a fancy, a wealth of elaboration, and also an intellectual tension which form part of the mannerist synthesis, but he also admits that the term is insufficient to define the substance of Palladio's art and that the crisis of Renaissance values present in Mannerism appears only partially in his work.

[208] PANE, 1962, p. 16; PANE, 1961 (I), p. 64.

[209] PALLUCCHINI, 1959, p. 38.

BIBLIOGRAPHY

1550   G. VASARI, *Le vite de' più eccellenti Architetti Pittori e Scultori italiani*, Florence.

1555   A. F. DONI, *Seconda Libraria*, Venice.

1570   A. PALLADIO, *I Quattro Libri dell'Architettura*, Venice.

1571   G. B. MAGANZA, *Herculana in lingua venetiana nella vittoria dell'armata christiana contra Turchi*, Venice.

1575   F. SANSOVINO, *Ritratto delle più nobili et famose città d'Italia...*, Venice.

1603   C. RIPA, *Iconologia*, Rome (v. 1764-67 ed.).

1628   S. CASTELLINI, " La descritione della città di Vicenza," MS, Vicenza, Biblioteca Bertoliana, Libreria Gonzati 22.11.15, c. 292b (v. 1885 ed.).

1676   M. BOSCHINI, *I gioieli pittoreschi, virtuoso ornamento della città di Vicenza*, Venice.

1681   F. BALDINUCCI, *Notizie dei professori del disegno da Cimabue in qua*, Florence.

1704   P. A. ORLANDI, *Abecedario pittorico... (contenente le notizie de' Professori di pittura scultura ed Architettura)*, Bologna.

1715   G. LEONI, *L'architettura di Andrea Palladio in inglese, italiano e francese, con note ed osservazioni di Innico Jones, riveduta, disegnata e pubblicata da Giacomo Leoni*, London.

1721   G. LEONI, *The Architecture of Andrea Palladio, in Four Books*, London.

1730   R. BURLINGTON, *Fabbriche antiche disegnate da Andrea Palladio Vicentino e date in luce da Richard Burlington*, London.

1740   F. MUTTONI (I), *Architettura di Andrea Palladio di nuovo ristampata... con le osservazioni dell'architetto N. N. e la traduzione francese*, Venice.

       F. MUTTONI (II), "Dissegni e Annotationi fatte di commissione del signor K.re Tomaso Tuixden Inglese, da F. M. attuale architetto della Città di Vicenza, con lui fatte delli Palazzi eretti sopra Dissegni ideati dal celebre Andrea Palladio, come in sua pubblicatione l'anno (1740)," n.p. (MS in the Library of the Centro Internazionale di Studi di Architettura " A. Palladio," Vicenza).

1749   G. MONTENARI, *Discorso del Teatro Olimpico del Palladio in Vicenza*, Padua.

1761   O. BERTOTTI SCAMOZZI, *Il forestiere istrutto nelle cose più rare di Architettura e di alcune Pitture della città di Vicenza*, Vicenza.

1762   T. TEMANZA, *Vita di Andrea Palladio vicentino*, Venice.

1764-67   C. RIPA, *Iconologia del Cavaliere Cesare Ripa Perugino notabilmente accresciuta d'Immagini, di Annotazioni e di Fatti dall'Abate Cesare Orlandi...*, Perugia (v. 1603 ed.).

1768   F. MILIZIA, *Memorie degli architetti*, Bologna.

1776-83   O. BERTOTTI SCAMOZZI (I), *Le fabbriche e i disegni di Andrea Palladio raccolti ed illustrati*, ed. F. Modena, Vicenza (v. 1786 ed.).

       O. BERTOTTI SCAMOZZI (II), *Les bâtiments et les dessins de André Palladio recueillis et illustrés par O. Bertotti Scamozzi*, Vicenza.

1776-1804   J. T. FACCIOLI, *Musaeum Lapidarium Vicentinum*, Vicenza.

1778   T. TEMANZA, *Le vite dei più celebri architetti e scultori veneziani del sec. XVI*, Venice (v. 1966 ed.).

1779   P. BALDARINI, *Descrizione delle architetture, pitture e scolture di Vicenza*, Vicenza.

       F. V. MOSCA, *Descritione delle architetture pitture e sculture di Vicenza*, Vicenza.

1782   G. B. GIOVIO, *Elogio di Palladio*, Padua (included in *Elogi italiani*, Venice, n. d., XI, iv).

1785   O. BERTOTTI SCAMOZZI, *Le terme dei Romani disegnate da Andrea Palladio e ripubblicate con la giunta di alcune osservazioni da Ottavio Bertotti Scamozzi giusta l'esemplare del lord conte di Burlington*, Vicenza (v. 1797 ed.).

1786   O. BERTOTTI SCAMOZZI, *Le fabbriche e i disegni di Andrea Palladio raccolti ed illustrati*, Vicenza (v. 1776-83 ed.).

1787   F. MILIZIA, *Dizionario delle belle arti del disegno*, II.

1797   O. BERTOTTI SCAMOZZI, *Le terme dei Romani...* (v. 1785 ed.), 2nd. ed. B. Rossi, Vicenza.

1810   L. CICOGNARA, "Elogio di Andrea Palladio," in *Discorsi letti nella Regale Veneta Accademia di Antichità e Belle Arti nell'agosto MDCCCX*, Venice.

1818   G. GALEANI NAPIONE, "Vita di Andrea Palladio," in *Vite ed elogi d'illustri italiani*, III, Pisa.

1822   G. B. BERTI, *Guida per Vicenza*, Venice.

1826-34   E. CICOGNA, *Iscrizioni veneziane*, Venice.

1830   A. C. QUATREMÈRE DE QUINCY, *Histoire de la vie et des ouvrages des plus célèbres architectes*, II, Paris.

1837   C. RIDOLFI, *Le meraviglie dell'arte, ovvero le vite degli illustri pittori veneti e dello stato*, Padua (Ist. ed. 1646; 2nd. ed. 1648; D. F. von Hadeln, Berlin, 1914).

1842-44   A. C. QUATREMÈRE DE QUINCY, *Dictionnaire historique d'architecture*, Paris.

1845   A. MAGRINI, *Dell'architettura in Vicenza, discorso con appendice critico-cronologica delle principali sue fabbriche negli ultimi otto secoli*, Padua.

1845-46   A. MAGRINI, *Memorie intorno la vita e le opere di Andrea Palladio*, Padua.

1847   G. PULLÉ, *Album di gemme architettoniche, ossia gli edi-fizii più rimarchevoli di Vicenza e del suo territorio, rilevati da Giuseppe Zanetti, disegnati da Marco Moro e con cenni illustrativi dimostrati da Giulio co. Pullé,* Venice.

1851   A. MAGRINI, *Cenni storico-critici sulla vita e sulle opere di Giovanni Antonio Fasolo pittore vicentino,* Venice.

1855   J. BURCKHARDT, *Der Cicerone, eine Anleitung zum Genuss der Kunstwerke Italiens,* Basle, 1855 (v. 1952 ed.).

       A. MAGRINI, *Il Palazzo del Museo Civico in Vicenza de-scritto ed illustrato,* Vicenza.

1880   C. BOITO, *Terzo centenario di A. Palladio* (lecture), Vicenza.

       D. BORTOLAN - F. LAMPERTICO, *Dei nomi delle contrade nella città di Vicenza,* Vicenza.

       F. LAMPERTICO, " Su Andrea Palladio." Lecture given to the Società di Mutuo Soccorso degli Artigiani Vicentini at the Rotonda on 19 September 1880, Florence; extract from *Archivio Storico Italiano,* s. 4, vol. VI.

       P. MOLMENTI, *Storia di Venezia nella vita privata,* II, Turin.

       G. VASARI, "Vita di fra' Giocondo e di altri Veronesi," in *Opere,* Florence.

       G. ZANELLA, *Vita di Andrea Palladio,* Milan.

1881   A. NEGRIN, *Del ristauro della Loggia del Capitanio ora resi-denza municipale nella Piazza dei Signori di Vicenza,* Vi-cenza (v. DE MORI, 1932).

1883   C. BOITO, *Leonardo, Michelangelo, Palladio,* Milan.

1885   S. CASTELLINI, *La descritione della città di Vicenza,* ed. D. Bortolan (v. 1628 ms).

1886   G. BIADEGO, *Nuovi documenti sopra Andrea Palladio,* Ve-rona.

1888   F. MONZA, *Cronaca,* Vicenza.

1890   P. DE NOLHAC - A. SOLERTI, *Il viaggio in Italia di Enrico III,* Turin.

1892   D. BORTOLAN, *L'antica Loggia del Palazzo del Capitanio in Vicenza,* Vicenza.

1902   B. F. FLETCHER, *Andrea Palladio, his Life and Works,* London.

1903   A. DE FILIPPI, " I monumenti palladiani a Vicenza," in *Cosmos illustrato.*

1905   R. BLOMFIELD, *Studies in Architecture,* London.

1908   R. PREDELLI, "Le Memorie e le carte di Alessandro Vit-toria," in *Archivio Trentino,* XXIII, fasc. 1-2, II.

1909   W. J. ANDERSON, *The Architecture of the Renaissance in Italy,* London.

       J. BURGER, *Die Villen des Andrea Palladio,* Leipzig.

       G. G. ZORZI, "La soluzione di un problema a proposito della Loggia del Capitaniato," in *La provincia di Vicenza,* Vicenza.

1910   L. ONGARO, "Il riordinamento del Museo Civico," in *Bol-lettino del Museo Civico di Vicenza,* January-March.

1912   G. PETTINA, *Vicenza,* Bergamo.

1914   C. GURLITT, *Andrea Palladio,* Berlin.

1915   G. FIOCCO, *Introduzione alla vita di fra' Giocondo ed altri veronesi scritta da G. Vasari,* Florence.

1916   G. FIOCCO, "Giovanni Giocondo veronese," Verona (extract from the *Atti dell'Accademia di Agricoltura di Verona,* s. 4, XVI, 1915).

1919   A. E. BRINCKMANN, *Die Baukunst des XVII. und XVIII. Jahrhunderts in der Romanischen Ländern,* Berlin.

1921   G. VINACCIA, *I maestri dell'architettura: Andrea Palladio,* Turin.

1921-22 C. ANTI, "L'arco dei Gavi a Verona," in *Architettura e Arti decorative,* I.

1922   G. G. ZORZI, "La vera origine e la giovanezza di Andrea Palladio," in *Archivio Storico veneto tridentino,* II, Trent.

1923   C. RICCI, *L'architettura del Cinquecento in Italia,* Turin.

1924   G. LOUKOMSKI, *Andrea Palladio,* Munich (v. 1927 ed.).

       A. VENTURI, *Storia dell' arte italiana: L' architettura del Quattrocento,* Vol. VIII, pt. ii, Milan.

1925   G. G. ZORZI, "Contributo alla storia dell'arte vicentina nei secoli XV e XVI," in *Miscellanea di studi e memorie della Deputazione di Storia Patria delle Venezie,* pt. iii.

1926   A. M. BRIZIO, "Per una definizione critica di Paolo Vero-nese," in *L'Arte,* XXIX.

1927   G. K. LOUKOMSKI (I), *Andrea Palladio,* Paris (v. 1924 ed.).

       G. K. LOUKOMSKI (II), "The Palaces of Palladio," in *Apol-lo,* VI.

1928   G. M. CANTACUZÈNE, *Palladio, essai critique,* Bucharest.

       G. FRANCESCHINI, "Cronache vicentine: il completamento della 'Loggia del Capitaniato' di Andrea Palladio," in *Em-porium,* no. 67.

       A. MELANI, *Palladio (1508-80), la sua vita e la sua arte, la sua influenza,* Milan.
       Per il completamento della Loggia del Capitaniato, Vicenza (publ. by the Commune di Vicenza).

1930   G. C. ARGAN, "Andrea Palladio e la critica neoclassica," in *L'Arte,* XXXIII.

       G. FASOLO, *Note d'arte,* Vicenza.

1931   R. BRENZONI, "Francesco Muttoni," in U. Thieme - F. Bec-ker, *Allgemeines Lexicon der bildenden Künstler von der Antike bis zur Gegenwart,* XXV, Leipzig.

1932   G. DE MORI, *Vicenza e la sua provincia, guida turistica,* Vicenza.

       H. WILLICH, "Andrea Palladio," in Thieme-Becker, *Allge-meines Lexicon,* XXVI.

1933   G. FIOCCO (I), *Andrea Palladio padovano,* Padua.

       G. FIOCCO (II), "Fra' Giovanni Giocondo," in *Enciclope-dia Italiana,* XVII, Milan-Rome.

       E. MICHALSKI, "Das Problem des Manierismus in der ita-lienischen Architektur," in *Zeitschrift für Kunstgeschichte,* II, fasc. 2.

1934-35 E. GOMBRICH, "Zum Werke Giulio Romanos," in *Jahr-buch der kunsthistorischen Sammlungen in Wien,* nos. 8-9.

1935   L. BROSCH, " G. M. Falconetto, 1535-1935," in *Le Tre Ve-nezie,* no. 4.

       G. GIOVANNONI (I), "Andrea Palladio," in *Enciclopedia Italiana,* XXVI, Milan-Rome.

       G. GIOVANNONI (II), *Lezioni sugli stili architettonici,* Rome, n. d. (1935?).

1936   L. BECHERUCCI, *Architettura italiana del Cinquecento,* Flor-ence.

1937   G. G. ZORZI, "Contributo alla storia dell'arte vicentina dei secoli XV e XVI: il preclassicismo e i pre-palladiani," in *Miscellanea di Studi e Memorie della Deputazione di Storia Patria delle Venezie,* pt. ii.

1938   G. FASOLO, "Notizie d'arte e di storia vicentina," in *Archivio Veneto*, s. 5, XXII.

V. TRETTENERO, *Andrea Palladio scrittore*, Milan.

A. VENTURI, *Storia dell'arte italiana: Scultura del Cinquecento*, vol. X, pt. iii, Milan.

1939   G. GIOVANNONI, "Quesiti di restauro: la Loggia del Capitaniato di Vicenza," in *Palladio*, III.

J. SCOTT, *Architettura dell'Umanesimo*, Bari (Engl. ed., *The Architecture of Humanism*, 1st ed. 1914).

1940   A. VENTURI, *Storia dell'arte italiana: Architettura del Cinquecento*, vol. XI, pt. iii, Milan.

1941   A. M. DALLA POZZA, *Palladiana*, Vicenza.

H. PÉE, *Die Palastbauten des Andrea Palladio*, Würzburg.

1942   G. C. ARGAN, "Cultura artistica della fine del Cinquecento," in *Le Arti*.

1943   A. M. DALLA POZZA, *Palladio*, Vicenza.

N. PEVSNER, *An Outline of European Architecture*, Harmondsworth (v. 1959 and 1963 eds.).

1944   R. PALLUCCHINI, *La pittura veneziana del Cinquecento*, Novara.

1946   B. CROCE, *La critica e la storia delle arti figurative*, Bari.

1948   R. PANE, *Andrea Palladio*, Turin (v. 1961 ed.).

L. VENTURI, *Storia della critica d'arte*, Florence (v. 1964 ed.).

B. ZEVI, *E. G. Asplund*, Milan.

1949   S. BETTINI, "La critica dell'architettura e l'arte di Palladio," in *Arte Veneta*, III.

G. FIOCCO, "L'esposizione dei disegni di Andrea Palladio a Vicenza," in *Arte Veneta*, III.

E. FRANCIA, "Palladio al vaglio di quattro secoli," in *Centenario palladiano* (1549-1949, publ. by the Banca Cattolica del Veneto).

A. NAVA, "La teoria di Viollet-le-Duc e 'l'architettura funzionale'," in *Critica d'Arte*, VIII.

G. G. ZORZI, "Ancora della vera origine e della giovinezza di Andrea Palladio secondo nuovi documenti," in *Arte Veneta*, III.

1950   L. MAGAGNATO, "La mostra dei disegni del Palladio a Vicenza," in *Emporium*, LVI.

G. NICCO FASOLA, "Manierismo e Architettura," in *Studi Vasariani*, Florence.

1951   G. G. ZORZI, "Alessandro Vittoria a Vicenza e lo scultore Lorenzo Rubini," in *Arte Veneta*, V.

1952   F. BARBIERI, "Un interprete settecentesco del Palladio: Ottavio Bertotti-Scamozzi," in *Palladio*, n. s., I.

J. BURCKHARDT, *Il Cicerone, guida al godimento dell'arte in Italia*, Florence, transl. F. Pfister (v. 1855 ed.).

L. MAGAGNATO, " I 'taiapietra' in Vicenza," in *Prima Mostra della Pietra di Vicenza* (catalogue), Venice.

1953   A. BARDELLA, *Memorie vicentine*, Vicenza.

R. PANE, *Bernini architetto*, Venice.

1953-54   R. BRENZONI, "Nuovi dati d'archivio sul Falconetto e su Bartolomeo e Ottaviano Ridolfi," in *Atti dell'Istituto Veneto di Scienze Lettere e Arti*, CXVI, Venice.

1954   C. PEROGALLI, *Monumenti e metodi di valorizzazione*, Milan.

R. WITTKOWER, "Giacomo Leoni's edition of Palladio's Quattro Libri dell'Architettura," in *Arte Veneta*, VIII.

G. G. ZORZI, "Progetti giovanili di Andrea Palladio per palazzi e case in Venezia e in terraferma," in *Palladio*, n.s. IV, fasc. 3.

1955   G. G. ZORZI, "Contributo alla datazione di alcune opere palladiane," in *Arte Veneta*, IX.

1956   G. C. ARGAN, "L'importanza del Sanmicheli nella formazione del Palladio," in *Venezia e l'Europa, Atti del XVIII Congresso Internazionale di Storia dell'Arte*, Venice.

F. BARBIERI - R. CEVESE - L. MAGAGNATO, *Guida di Vicenza*, Vicenza.

A. CHASTEL, *L'art italien*, Paris (v. 1958 ed.).

A. HAUSER, *Storia sociale dell'arte*, Turin.

R. PANE, "Andrea Palladio e la interpretazione dell'architettura rinascimentale," in *Venezia e l'Europa, Atti del XVIII Congresso Internazionale di Storia dell'Arte*, Venice.

N. PEVSNER, "Palladio and Europe," in *Venezia e l'Europa, Atti del XVIII Congresso Internazionale di Storia dell'Arte*, Venice.

1958   A. CHASTEL, *L'arte italiana*, Florence (v. 1956 ed.).

T. PIGNATTI, "Andrea Palladio e Paolo Veronese," in *Storia dell'arte italiana* (in collaboration with G. MAZZARIOL), Milan-Verona.

J. SUMMERSON, *Architecture in Britain (1530-1830)*, Harmondsworth.

1958-59   P. GUALDO, " Vita di Andrea Palladio," ed. G. G. ZORZI, in *Saggi e memorie di Storia dell'Arte*, II.

1959   L. CREMA, *L'architettura romana*, Turin (vol. XII, pt. I of the *Enciclopedia Classica*).

G. FIOCCO, Introduction to G. G. ZORZI, *I disegni delle antichità di Palladio*, Venice.

P. FRANCASTEL, *L'arte e la civiltà moderna*, Milan.

L. GRASSI, *Camillo Boito*, Milan.

R. PALLUCCHINI, "Andrea Palladio e Giulio Romano," in *Bollettino del Centro Internazionale di Studi di Architettura A. Palladio*, I.

R. PANE (I), *Città antiche edilizia nuova*, Naples.

R. PANE (II), "La formazione del Palladio e il Manierismo," in *Bollettino del Centro Internazionale di Studi di Architettura A. Palladio*, I.

R. WITTKOWER, "Diffusione dei modi palladiani in Inghilterra," in *Bollettino del Centro Internazionale di Studi di Architettura A. Palladio*, I.

B. ZEVI, "Sanmicheli: attualità del suo insegnamento sincretico," in *L'architettura, cronache e storia*, V, no. 47.

G. G. ZORZI, *I disegni delle antichità di Andrea Palladio*, Venice.

1960   E. BATTISTI, *Rinascimento e barocco*, Turin.

A. M. BRIZIO, "La pittura di Paolo Veronese in rapporto con l'opera del Sanmicheli e del Palladio," in *Bollettino del Centro Internazionale di Studi di Architettura A. Palladio*, II.

C. BRANDI (I), " Perché Palladio non è neoclassico," in *Bollettino del Centro Internazionale di Studi di Architettura A. Palladio*, II.

C. BRANDI (II), *Segno e immagine*, Milan.

A. CHASTEL, "Palladio et l'art des fêtes," in *Bollettino del Centro Internazionale di Studi di Architettura A. Palladio*, II.

E. LAVAGNINO, *Ia chiesa di S. Spirito in Sassia: il mutare del gusto a Roma al tempo del Concilio di Trento*, Turin.

W. Timofiewitsch, "Die Palladio-Forschung in den Jahren von 1940 bis 1960," in *Zeitschrift für Kunstgeschichte*, XXIII, no. 2.

R. Wittkower, "L'architettura di Lord Burlington (1694-1753) e del suo ambiente," in *Bollettino del Centro Internazionale di Studi di Architettura A. Palladio*, II.

B. Zevi, *Architettura in nuce*, Venice-Rome.

M. Zocca, "Le concezioni urbanistiche di Palladio," in *Palladio*, n. s. X.

1961   F. Barbieri, "Un'opera pressoché ignorata di G. A. Fasolo: le tele per la Loggia del Capitaniato a Vicenza," in *Arte Veneta*, XV.

S. Bettini (I), "Palladio urbanista," in *Arte Veneta*, XV.

S. Bettini (II), "Palladio urbanista," in *Bollettino del Centro Internazionale di Studi di Architettura A. Palladio*, III.

G. Canova, "I viaggi di Paris Bordone," in *Arte Veneta*, XV.

G. E. Ferrari, "Schede di bibliografia palladiana dal 1955," in *Bollettino del Centro Internazionale di Studi di Architettura A. Palladio*, III.

E. Forssman, *Palladios Lehrgebäude*, Uppsala (v. 1965 ed.).

W. Lotz, "Mannerism in Architecture: Changing Aspects," in *The Renaissance and Mannerism, Acts of the XX International Congress of the History of Art*, Princeton, 1961.

R. Pane (I), *Andrea Palladio*, Turin (v. 1948 ed.).

R. Pane (II), "Invenzione e restauro nella basilica palladiana," in *Bollettino del Centro Internazionale di Studi di Architettura A. Palladio*, III.

C. Semenzato, "Giovan Maria Falconetto," in *Bollettino del Centro Internazionale di Studi di Architettura A. Palladio*, III.

A. Venditti, *Architettura neoclassica a Napoli*, Naples.

G. G. Zorzi, "Giovanni Antonio Fasolo, pittore lombardo-vicentino, emulo di Paolo Veronese," in *Arte Lombarda*, VI.

1962   E. Arslan, "Postilla a un articolo su Giovanni Antonio Fasolo," in *Arte Lombarda*, VII, pt. 1.

A. Blunt, *Artistic Theory in Italy*, Oxford (rpt. 1966; 1st ed. 1940).

M. Bolzonella, "Gian Maria Falconetto," in *Città di Padova*, II, no. 6.

R. Cevese, review of R. Pane, *Palladio*, in *Bollettino del Centro Internazionale di Studi di Architettura A. Palladio*, IV.

R. De Fusco, "E. E. Viollet-le-Duc," in *Comunità*, no. 105.

F. Franco (I), "Francesco Muttoni: l'architetto di Vicenza N. N.," in *Bollettino del Centro Internazionale di Studi di Architettura A. Palladio*, IV.

F. Franco (II), "Il *Palladio* di Roberto Pane," in *Arte Veneta*, XVI.

R. Pane, "Palladio e la critica," in *Bollettino del Centro Internazionale di Studi di Architettura A. Palladio*, IV.

G. Weise, "Storia del termine Manierismo," in *Convegno Internazionale dell'Accademia dei Lincei (Manierismo, Barocco, Rococò: concetti e termini)*, Rome.

R. Wittkower, *Architectural Principles in the Age of Humanism*, London, 3rd rev. ed. (rpt. New York, 1965; 1st ed. 1949).

1963   F. Franco, "Ottavio Bertotti-Scamozzi," in *Bollettino del Centro Internazionale di Studi di Architettura A. Palladio*, V.

G. Lorenzetti, *Venezia e il suo estuario*, Rome.

G. Lorenzoni, "Giorgio Fossati, le cosiddette opere inedite palladiane e 'l'idea Palladio'," in *Padova e la sua provincia*, IX, n. s., nos. 1-2.

N. Pevsner, *An Outline of European Architecture*, Harmondsworth, 7th ed. (v. 1943 and 1959 eds.).

L. Puppi, *Il Teatro Olimpico*, Venice.

G. G. Zorzi (I), "La problematica palladiana in relazione alle più recenti scoperte," in *Bollettino del Centro Internazionale di Studi di Architettura A. Palladio*, V.

G. G. Zorzi (II), "Seconda postilla a un articolo su Giovan Antonio Fasolo e il suo testamento," in *Arte Lombarda*, VIII, pt. 2.

1964   F. Barbieri (I), "Palladio e il manierismo," in *Bollettino del Centro Internazionale di Studi di Architettura A. Palladio*, VI.

F. Barbieri (II), review of E. Forssman, *Palladios Lehrgebäude*, in *Bollettino del Centro Internazionale di Studi di Architettura A. Palladio*, VI.

L. Becherucci, "Mannerism," *Encyclopedia of World Art*, IX, cols. 443-478.

R. Cevese, review of G. G. Zorzi, *Le opere pubbliche e i palazzi privati di A. Palladio*, in *Bollettino del Centro Internazionale di Studi di Architettura A. Palladio*, VI, pt. 2.

M. Guiotto, "Recenti restauri di edifici palladiani," in *Bollettino del Centro Internazionale di Studi di Architettura A. Palladio*, VI, pt. 2.

R. Pane (I), "Palladio e la moderna storiografia dell'architettura," in *Bollettino del Centro Internazionale di Studi di Architettura A. Palladio*, VI.

R. Pane (II), *Anton Gaudì*, Milan.

L. Venturi, *History of Art Criticism*, transl. C. Mariott, New York (v. 1948 ed.).

B. Zevi, "Attualità di Michelangiolo architetto," in *Michelangiolo architetto*, ed. P. Portoghesi and B. Zevi, Turin.

1964-65 R. Pane, "Teoria della conservazione e del restauro dei monumenti," in *Napoli Nobilissima*, s. 3, IV.

1965   R. Cevese, "Appunti palladiani," in *Bollettino del Centro Internazionale di Studi di Architettura A. Palladio*, VII.

A. Chastel, "Palladio et l'escalier," in *Bollettino del Centro Internazionale di Studi di Architettura A. Palladio*, VII.

G. E. Ferrari, "Schede di bibliografia palladiana del quinquennio 1961-1965," in *Bollettino del Centro Internazionale di Studi di Architettura A. Palladio*, VII.

E. Forssman, *Palladios Lehrgebäude*, Stockholm, 2nd ed. (v. 1961 ed.).

A. Hauser, *Il manierismo: la crisi del Rinascimento e l'origine dell'arte moderna*, Turin.

E. Tafuri, "Il parco della villa Trissino a Trissino e l'opera di Francesco Muttoni," in *L'architettura, cronache e storia*, X, no. 114.

G. G. Zorzi (I), *Le opere pubbliche e i palazzi privati di Andrea Palladio*, Venice.

G. G. Zorzi (II), "Un nuovo soggiorno di Alessandro Vittoria nel Vicentino: i suoi rapporti con Lorenzo Rubini e i suoi figli," in *Arte Veneta*, XIX.

1966   J. S. Ackerman, *Palladio*, Harmondsworth.

E. Forssman, "Falconetto e Palladio," in *Bollettino del Centro Internazionale di Studi di Architettura A. Palladio*, VIII.

W. Lotz, " Riflessioni sul tema Palladio urbanista," in *Bollettino del Centro Internazionale di Studi di Architettura A. Palladio*, VIII.

M. Tafuri, *L'architettura del Manierismo nel Cinquecento Europeo*, Rome.

T. Temanza, *Le vite dei più celebri architetti e scultori veneziani del secolo XVI*, with a critical essay by Liliana Grassi, Milan (v. 1778 ed.).

B. Zevi (I), "Andrea Palladio," *Encyclopedia of World Art*, XI, cols. 59-81.

B. Zevi (II), " Michele Sanmicheli," *Encyclopedia of World Art*, XII, cols. 691-700.

1967 E. Battisti, " Storia del concetto di manierismo in architettura," in *Bollettino del Centro Internazionale di Studi di Architettura A. Palladio*, IX.

A. Hauser, " L'ambiente spirituale del manierismo," in *Bollettino del Centro Internazionale di Studi di Architettura A. Palladio*, IX.

W. Lotz, " Palladio e Sansovino," in *Bollettino del Centro Internazionale di Studi di Architettura A. Palladio*, IX.

N. Pevsner, " Palladio e il manierismo," in *Bollettino del Centro Internazionale di Studi di Architettura A. Palladio*, IX.

C. Semenzato (I), "Gli spazi esterni e il manierismo di Andrea Palladio," in *Bollettino del Centro Internazionale di Studi di Architettura A. Palladio*, IX.

C. Semenzato (II), " Jacopo Sansovino," in *Bollettino del Centro Internazionale di Studi di Architettura A. Palladio*, IX.

A. Venditti, *Architettura bizantina nell'Italia Meridionale*, Naples.

G. G. Zorzi, "Urbanistica palladiana," in *Bollettino del Centro Internazionale di Studi di Architettura A. Palladio*, IX.

1968 F. Barbieri, *La Basilica Palladiana*, Vicenza (v. 1970 ed.).

R. De Fusco, *Il codice dell'architettura: antologia di trattatisti*, Naples.

1970 F. Barbieri, *The Basilica of Andrea Palladio*, University Park (v. 1968 ed.).

THE PICTORIAL DECORATION

FRANCO BARBIERI

THE PICTORIAL DECORATION

The ceiling of the hall has been restored to its original aspect: the wooden coffers "alla ducale" adorned with modillions and rosettes and the large beams with geometric designs in dark red on a monochrome ground are from the late Cinquecento, painstakingly restored in 1960.[1] Nine paintings depicting episodes from Roman history decorate the spaces between the beams. They were removed at some point between 1822 and 1830 when the ceiling was extensively repaired, but were restored and replaced in 1961 (Plates 50-51).[2]

The three main scenes are placed along the middle axis (the paintings measure 4 x 4 meters). In the center is Mutius Scaevola placing his hand in the fire as he stands before Porsenna (Plate 53); on the left, looking from the entrance, Marcus Curtius plunges into the chasm (Plate 52), and on the right is Horatius Cocles defending the bridge (Plate 54). The six smaller scenes (4 x 2 meters) along the sides are not so easily identified, apart from that of Titus Manlius Torquatus slaying the Gaul, who lies at his feet (Plate 57),[3] now in the left corner of the south side facing Piazza dei Signori.

As far back as Ridolfi, all the sources agree in attributing these pictures to Giovanni Antonio Fasolo. Only Castellini, writing around 1628, assigns them to Paolo Veronese.[4] But there can be no doubt whatsoever about the attribution proposed " ab antiquo," so many and obvious are the signs of Fasolo's manner, although as Boschini has said, and as is appropriate here as well, the work is " segnato col carattere di Paolo Veronese." But indeed, Fasolo is very different in the pomposity of his compositions, which show typically mannerist schemes but are enlivened according to the artist's particular style with a robust, instinctively coloristic vein.[5] The huge, heavy figures in the foreground, who play their parts with solemn gestures emphasizing the regal oratory, are the authentic stamp of the author. They are painted with that vigorous "formalism of sculptural relief that had been much appreciated in Verona," [6] which goes back to the Mantuans steeped in Giulio Romano. The dense, oily color—insofar as it can be appreciated after the restorations—is peculiarly well-adapted to the impressively full-bodied figures; within these limits the heads, although diminished by foreshortening, show that we are dealing with a first-class portrait painter.

There is little difficulty in fixing the chronology of the paintings. The last payment for the roof over the Loggia del Capitaniato, which was reconstructed accord-ing to Palladio's plan with amazing speed between April and December 1571, dates to February 1572.[7] On the following May 5th, the sum necessary for finishing the work was allotted by a deliberation of the commission supervising the building operations.[8] Magrini, followed by other critics who interpret the documents somewhat broadly, believes that this deliberation must refer to the execution of the paintings.[9] In any case, Fasolo died when he was just over forty years old, on 23 August 1572,[10] as a result of falling from a scaffold while he was finishing the series of Roman history scenes; modern restoration and research has shown that they were painted *in situ*.[11] By that time the series must have been finished, since Fasolo's own hand is undeniably present, notwithstanding the doubts that have been expressed.[12]

We therefore have an important date with which to understand the direction of Fasolo's taste in its last phase, in the sense of perspective decoration.[13] When compared with the "subdued" space and measured against the frescoes in Villa Caldogno Pagello at Caldogno, painted somewhat earlier (around 1570),[14] the scenes in the Loggia certainly show that the painter was evolving toward that more complex, elaborate, and evocative phase of perspective decoration which he shared with other members of the late circle of Veronese.[15]

Attention should be drawn, however, not only to the spectacular "sottinsù" effect which dramatizes these massive, tumbling bodies,[16] but also—once the somewhat vacuous theatricality is accepted—to the sensuous and elongated figures sketched with facile rapidity against the vast backgrounds. In these examples of his last work, Fasolo really seems to have abandoned the sensually realistic note that stamped his manner: the figures in the frescoes at Caldogno—evoked with such powerful realism within the fantastically mannerist decorative structures that they become almost "existential" [17]—have given way through nervous touches of color to sinuous, gleaming apparitions.

Consider, for example, the figures crowding together at the top of the stairs around the high priest in the episode of Marcus Curtius (Plate 52): within a violently dramatic atmosphere, among flowing beards and faces marked by deep, hollow eyes, a head reduced to a grotesque mask suddenly appears at the extreme edge of the flight of steps. Some of the artist's more experimental, exaggerated figures are to be found among the crowd gathered below the vast architectural settings of his

Piscina Probatica [18] in the Pinacoteca in Vicenza: this is another late work, in which Venturi has remarked on " lo sforzo del comporre sonante." [19]

It is exactly in episodes such as these that the mannerist traits elsewhere inflated by academic bombast have been freed from the bonds that shackled them and interpreted according to a more liberal form of the intuitive imagination. [20] The consequences were to be both profound and immediate in the Vicentine circle. In fact, if there were any doubt at all about the sources informing us that Alessandro Maganza began his education as a painter when still in his early youth in Fasolo's studio, [21] these paintings in the Loggia del Capitaniato would serve to dismiss it.

In 1572 Maganza was just sixteen years old and had not yet come into direct contact with the influential world of Venice. He was to do so shortly after his master's death, when his mind was already conditioned to some extent by the visionary and sinuous tone of Fasolo's Loggia scenes, as some of his own paintings and those of his son Giambattista clearly show. It was in Alessandro Maganza's atelier that Fasolo's achievements were perpetuated; the haunting atmosphere of his paintings merging with the luminosity typical of Maganza's own work anticipate some of the best paintings of Francesco Maffei. [22]

According to Gonzati, [23] the hall of the Loggia was also decorated with a fresco frieze by Fasolo, but this had already vanished when Gonzati was writing (about the middle of the nineteenth century). A discovery made in the summer of 1960 is interesting in this connection: several tests carried out on the plaster covering the walls revealed that the latter are out of plumb; this was customary in the past whenever walls were to be covered with frescoes. [24] It is therefore quite likely that there was a frescoed band around the room below the ceiling beams, probably of the type Fasolo must have painted between 1565 and 1567 for the hall of the Casa Cogollo, [25] and again much earlier (in about 1552) in the old Casa dei Montagna at San Lorenzo. [26] If we accept this hypothesis, it affords further evidence that the use of frescoed friezes or of friezes on canvas was very common in Vicenza in the Cinquecento and later in the Seicento, as a result of the great fashion for Mantuan decorative themes inspired by the Palazzo del Te. [27]

The walls of the hall (Plate 50) are now adorned with fragments of frescoes taken from a frieze in the Cinquecento villa di Paolina Porto at Torri di Quartesolo. [28] On entering we find the entrance wall and the one on the right adorned with battle scenes; in front are a pair of Cupids pouring water from a vase, and military trophies, banners, and weapons; on the left are Mars, and Minerva as the goddess of war. There are ten pieces in the series. These details from the frieze, along with other sections scattered about in other parts of the town hall [29] and on the main staircase of the Biblioteca Bertoliana, glorified the military feats of Ippolito Porto, a mercenary captain who was first in the service of the Duke of Savoy and the Emperor Charles V and later in that of the Venetian Republic, by which he was sent to act as governor of Corfu. He died there in 1572 [30] and was honored by a monument in the Church of San Lorenzo in Vicenza. [31]

Magrini attributed the frescoes to Giovanni Antonio Fasolo. [32] Later they were described as belonging to the school of Paolo Veronese; [33] the present writer is the first to have assigned them to the circle of Zelotti. [34] Crosato considers that the evident similarity between these historical episodes and those at the Castle of Cataio leads us to attribute the decoration to Zelotti and to exclude the presence of Fasolo. [35] Rupprecht denies this, maintaining that the frescoes are less than mediocre in quality. [36]

Indeed, the general level is not very high: often, as Crosato herself admits, the execution is weak, the drawing undistinguished, the forms heavy, the flesh dull, and the draperies like parchment; whereas the battle scenes betray a love of minute detail which does nothing to heighten the pictorial effect. [37] But this judgment, which is perhaps a little too severe, does not take into account certain rather good passages, such as the figures of Mars and Minerva; nor does it allow for the vicissitudes the whole series underwent, or for the participation of assistants, which was most likely extensive.

It is highly probable that the cycle was painted a little after the death of Ippolito Porto, whom it was to honor. Crosato suggests a date of 1572, [38] that is, when Zelotti was painting in his " new manner," a dry and metallic fashion which first appeared in about 1570 in the Cataio frescoes.

It is worth mentioning, finally, that Boschini and Baldarini, a century later, saw some paintings with " glorificazioni" of Venetian captains and rectors in the main hall and in other parts of the Loggia; however, these have completely disappeared, [39] together with a painting given to Paris Bordone mentioned as still in the Loggia at the beginning of the eighteenth century. [40]

NOTES

¹ BARIOLI, 1960, p. 134, states that during the summer the ceiling panels had to be reduced to their original dimensions, which was done by working on the six cornices running along the north and south sides. These had been reduced in width in the past for the sake of symmetry, by enlarging the imitation beams and reducing parts of the walls. It was a pleasant surprise to find that the beams and the original cornices had been largely preserved. See also GUIOTTO, 1964, p. 86.

² The date of their removal may be deduced from BERTI, who in 1822 (p. 30) stated that they were still *in situ* but in 1830 (p. 26) said that they were gone. The canvases, according to BARIOLI, 1960, p. 134, had been painted in place; they were stripped directly from their frames, and only a few were cut.

The first plan was to collect the paintings in the old Palazzo Comunale, adjacent to the Basilica; this building later became the seat of the Palazzo di Giustizia (see BARBIERI, 1953 [II] and 1956 [II]). But instead they were placed in the deconsecrated church of San Faustino (MAGRINI, 1851, pp. 41-44) and later (in 1834) were taken to the Pinacoteca Civica (MAGRINI, 1845, p. 167; ZANELLA, 1880, p. 73), which from 1832 was located in the hall of the Confraternita dei Rossi, above the Oratory of San Cristoforo (see MAGRINI, 1855 [II], p. 40, n. 6, and RUMOR, 1910, p. 4). The only person to protest against their removal was ALVERÀ, 1834, and in the " Notizie biografiche degli architetti vicentini." When the Pinacoteca and Museo were transferred to Palazzo Chiericati in 1855, the paintings were put into storage. Their locations in the Loggia were filled with nondescript decorations executed between 1850 and 1860: see LOUKOMSKI, 1924, p. 14, and esp. 1926, p. 69.

ONGARO, 1910, p. 7, suggested that the abandoned Roman scenes should at least be used in the ceiling of the hall in Palazzo Chiericati; PETTINA, 1912, p. 118, mentions them in his short essay on art in Vicenza; they are listed in THIEME-BECKER (1915), but with several inaccuracies, the author evidently not having checked the facts. In his edition of RIDOLFI (1648), von HADELN, 1924, p. 229, n. 3, notes regretfully that the paintings were probably ruined by then. Their history is somewhat confused from this time on: VENTURI, 1929, pp. 1011 and 1025, mentions only three, repeating the error RIDOLFI (1648, p. 234) had already made and with many inaccuracies; FASOLO, 1930, pp. 71-73, does not appear to have known where the paintings were; and PÉE, 1939, p. 144, calls them frescoes. Even the museum's inventories, including the last one made in 1950, fail to include them. As a consequence, in 1953 and 1956, when writing on the Loggia del Capitaniato for the guide to Vicenza, I also stated that they had been lost. They were quite unexpectedly rediscovered in April 1959 by dott. Andreina Ballerin, during work on parts of Palazzo Chiericati. Immediately afterward I identified and published them (1961).

The scenes were in very poor condition; from the very beginning, they had been unhappily located in the ceiling of the Loggia, for various reasons. BARIOLI, 1960, p. 134, says that since the canvases were not on stretchers they had sagged in the middle, and water leaking from the roof had collected in the hollows with disastrous results, thus justifying their removal. BALDARINI, 1799, pp. 19-21, had already complained of the damage to them, especially to the smaller ones; MAGRINI, 1851, pp. 41-44, confirmed that only the larger ones and one of the smaller ones were still legible. Nearly a century and a half of neglect while the paintings remained in storage had done the rest, causing great rents in the canvas and much rubbing of the

surfaces. Restoration was carried out in the summer of 1960 under the direction of Prof. Giuseppe Pedrocco, in the Gabinetto di Restauro of the Museo Civico in Vicenza. In order to set them in place again, part of the frames had to be remade and the roof rendered watertight. The paintings were mounted on wedged frames clamped to the ceiling panelling and surrounded with dovetailed wooden laths; the frame surrounding each picture was then given a waterproof plastic covering (BARIOLI, 1960, p. 134). Although we know nothing of the way in which the smaller pictures were arranged, BERTI, 1822, p. 30, following earlier sources, states that the scene of Mutius Scaevola, which is now in the center, was formerly on the left on entering the hall, and that of Marcus Curtius, which is now on the left, was in the center.

³ MAGRINI, 1851, pp. 41-44; authors rarely mention the subject of the smaller paintings, and some do not even list them at all (see note 4).

⁴ See CASTELLINI, " Descrizione della città di Vicenza," I, c. 292 b; 1885 ed., p. 124; RIDOLFI, 1648, p. 234 (lists only the three larger paintings); BOSCHINI, 1676, pp. 27-28, lists them all, as does BERTOTTI SCAMOZZI, 1761, pp. 22-23, and BALDARINI, 1779, pp. 19-21.

⁵ PALLUCCHINI, R., 1945, p. 105. On Giovanni Antonio Fasolo—who was born in 1530 in Mandello del Lario and lived and worked for many years in Vicenza, where he died in 1572—see ZORZI, 1961, and CROSATO, 1962, pp. 38-42 and list of artists, which includes a catalogue of Fasolo's frescoes in villas of the Veneto; see also the recent study by PALLUCCHINI, 1968, pp. 3-7, 19-20, 21-26.

⁶ SALMI, 1966, col. 120.

⁷ ZORZI, 1961, p. 224.

⁸ *Libri Partium*, III, c. 20 b.

⁹ MAGRINI, 1851, pp. 41-44; FASOLO, 1930, pp. 71-73. MAGRINI's previous statement (1845, Annotazioni, pp. liv-lv, n. 74) that he had not discovered any reference in the Vicentine archives to the pictures painted by Fasolo for the hall of the Loggia should also be borne in mind.

¹⁰ FACCIOLI, 1776, p. 144, n. 127, reproduces the painter's tombstone in the Church of San Michele in Vicenza, which was deconsecrated and demolished in 1812; the tombstone is now in San Lorenzo, in the second bay of the left aisle. It proves that RIDOLFI, 1648, p. 234, was mistaken when he said that Fasolo died at the age of 44.

¹¹ See note 2. Concerning RIDOLFI's error (1648, p. 235) in asserting that Fasolo had died while painting the frescoes in the audience chamber of the Palazzo del Podestà, where he had been working in 1567-68, see BARBIERI, 1961, p. 240, n. 27; ZORZI, 1961, pp. 219-220; and ZORZI, 1964, p. 113, n. 39. See also MAGRINI, 1851, p. 43, and ONGARO, 1926.

¹² MAGRINI, 1851, p. 43, believed that the artist left the six smaller canvases unfinished; ZORZI, 1961, p. 225, also insists on their uncompleted state. In any case, in 1572 the only person in Vicenza who would have been capable of finishing the job would have been Giambattista Maganza the Elder, who was just over sixty years old; however, his artistic personality is still too little understood for any plausible traces of his manner to be identifiable in these works: see LODI, 1965, pp. 108 and 116, nn. 1 and 2; BARBIERI, 1968 (II), pp. 48-49.

¹³ PALLUCCHINI, 1968, p. 26.

[14] CROSATO, 1962, p. 100; PALLUCCHINI, 1968, pp. 19 and 22.

[15] See DE MAFFEI, 1966, col. 230.

[16] PALLUCCHINI, 1968, p. 26.

[17] PALLUCCHINI, 1962, p. ix; 1968, pp. 22-23.

[18] FIOCCO, 1928, p. 47; VENTURI, 1929, p. 1025; BARBIERI, 1962, p. 71.

[19] VENTURI, 1932.

[20] See ARSLAN, 1947, p. 26, n. 19, who defines these more open motifs, which may also be found in other works by the painter, as his true hallmark.

[21] LODI, 1965, pp. 108-109 and n. 4.

[22] See PALLUCCHINI, A., 1945, p. 16.

[23] GONZATI, " Miscellanea storica vicentina."

[24] BARIOLI, 1960, p. 34.

[25] ZORZI, 1961, pp. 218-219; ZORZI, 1964, pp. 234-235. MAGAGNATO, 1953 and 1956, p. 159, and PALLUCCHINI, 1968, p. 26, cautiously concede that Fasolo may have been the author, but CROSATO, 1962, p. 37, is decidedly against this attribution and in favor of Zelotti. It must be remembered, however, that the frieze in the Casa Cogollo has been much altered by later changes and restorations.

[26] BARBIERI, 1964; I proposed a date for the frieze of the Casa Montagna very near to that of Fasolo's frescoes in the Castello Porto Colleoni di Thiene and assigned the latter to around 1550; see CROSATO, 1962, p. 195. Since it would seem more reasonable to date them around 1552 as PALLUCCHINI does (1968, p. 6), the frieze in the Casa Montagna I think should at any rate have to follow them.

[27] PALLUCCHINI, 1963, p. 340, n. 15. BARBIERI, 1964, pp. 199-200 and nn. 6-9 gives a brief survey of these Cinquecento and Seicento Vicentine friezes.

[28] For the exact identification of the villa, see ZORZI, 1963, pp. 118-119 and 1968, pp. 226-227, who attributes it to the "Palladian" activity of Domenico Groppino; FASOLO, 1929, pp. 83-84, and CEVESE, 1953, p. 93, also interested themselves in this building. For the reconstruction of the whole cycle of frescoes at Torri di Quartesolo and their present arrangement, see CROSATO, 1962, p. 198; MAGRINI, 1869, pp. 51-52, describes them as still

being *in situ*, but he was speaking mistakenly of a Villa Porto at Vancimuglio; FASOLO, 1929, p. 84, says that they were then already detached and kept in the Museo Civico.

[29] A large scene may be found in another small room adjacent to the hall of the Loggia.

[30] MAGRINI, 1869, pp. 20 and 50-52, discusses Ippolito Porto at some length.

[31] See ARSLAN, 1956, p. 125, n. 830.

[32] MAGRINI, 1851, pp. 40-42, and 1869, pp. 51-52.

[33] FASOLO, 1929, p. 84.

[34] BARBIERI, 1953 and 1956, p. 95.

[35] CROSATO, 1962, pp. 198-199.

[36] RUPPRECHT, 1962, p. 198.

[37] CROSATO, 1962, p. 199.

[38] CROSATO, 1962, pp. 37 and 198.

[39] According to BOSCHINI, 1676, pp. 26-28, in the hall of the Loggia, which he calls the " sala della audienza sopra la piazza," were "glorificazioni" of the captain Priamo da Lezze (G. Carpioni, 1665) and of the rectors Alvise Tron (A. Zanchi), Gerolamo Cornaro (P. Liberi), and Pietro Giustiniani (A. Maganza, 1614); in adjacent rooms (pp. 24-25) were those of the captains Caterino Bellegno (G. Carpioni, 1656) and Alvise Valier (P. Vecchia, 1634), of Agostino Nani (F. Maffei), and of the rector Giovanni Giustiniani (Baldassar Tedesco, 1631). BALDARINI, 1779, pp. 19-21, writing a century later, mentions only the three latter canvases in the hall of the Loggia. On the "glorificazioni" of Priamo da Lezze and Caterino Bellegno by Carpioni, see also PILO, 1961, pp. 67 and 135, who, however, mistakes the location and lists them as being at one time in the Palazzo del Podestà; see RICCOBONI, 1966, pp. 116-117 for the "glorificazione" of Alvise Tron.

[40] CHIUSOLE, 1782, p. 53, says that the badly deteriorated scene with the animals of the ark is a work by Paris Bordone, and a document shows that the painter received payment on 15 October 1521. See also PUPPI, 1963, pp. 383 and esp. 415-416, n. 44, on this painting by Bordone, which is sometimes listed as a fresco and as depicting a different subject, that of Noah's drunkenness. See also CANOVA, 1964, pp. 4 and 69; BARBIERI, 1970, p. 91, n. 252.

BIBLIOGRAPHY

MANUSCRIPT SOURCES (PUBLISHED OR UNPUBLISHED)

All the manuscripts are in the Biblioteca Bertoliana in Vicenza, Libreria Gonzati; therefore only the inventory number is given, in parenthesis.

S. CASTELLINI, "Descrizione della città di Vicenza dentro dalle mura e delli borghi della medesima," Vols. I-II, c. 1628 (22.11.15/16).

S. CASTELLINI, *Descrizione della città di Vicenza dentro dalle mura*, c. 1628, ed. D. BORTOLAN, Vicenza, 1885.

A. ALVERÀ, "Notizie biografiche degli architetti vicentini," 19th century (26.9.12).

L. GONZATI, "Miscellanea storica vicentina," 19th century (25.10.48).

Libri Partium del comune di Vicenza, Biblioteca Bertoliana, Archivio di Torre.

PUBLISHED SOURCES

1648 C. RIDOLFI, *Le meraviglie dell'Arte, ovvero le vite de gl'illustri pittori veneti e dello stato*, Vol. II, Venice (ed. D. F. VON HADELN, Berlin, 1924).

1676 M. BOSCHINI, *I gioieli pittoreschi virtuoso ornamento della città di Vicenza*, Venice.

1761 O. BERTOTTI SCAMOZZI, *Il Forestiere istrutto delle cose più rare di Architettura e di alcune pitture della città di Vicenza*, Vicenza.

1776 J. T. FACCIOLI, *Musaeum Lapidarium Vicentinum*, Vol. I, Vicenza.

1779 P. BALDARINI, *Descrizione delle architetture, pitture e sculture di Vicenza* (ed. E. ARNALDI, O. VECCHIA, L. BUFFETTI), Vol. II, Vicenza.

1782 A. CHIUSOLE, *Itinerario delle pitture, sculture ed architetture più rare di molte città d'Italia*, Vicenza.

1822 G. B. BERTI, *Guida per Vicenza*, Venice.

1830 G. B. BERTI, *Nuova guida per Vicenza*, Padua.

1834 A. ALVERÀ, *Le principali vedute di Vicenza e suoi dintorni con illustrazioni storiche*, Vicenza.

1845 A. MAGRINI, *Memorie intorno la vita e le opere di Andrea Palladio*, Padua.

1851 A. MAGRINI, *Cenni storico-critici sulla vita e sulle opere di Giovanni Antonio Fasolo pittore vicentino*, Venice.

1855 A. MAGRINI, *Il palazzo del Museo Civico in Vicenza descritto ed illustrato*, Vicenza.

A. MAGRINI (II), *Il Museo Civico di Vicenza solennemente inaugurato il 18 agosto 1855*, Vicenza.

1869 A. MAGRINI, *Reminiscenze vicentine della casa di Savoia*, Vicenza.

1880 G. ZANELLA, *Vita di Andrea Palladio*, Milan.

1910 L. ONGARO, "Il riordinamento del Museo Civico," in *Bollettino del Museo Civico di Vicenza*, fasc. 1 (January-March), pp. 7-10.

S. RUMOR, "Per la storia del nostro Museo," in *Bollettino del Museo Civico di Vicenza*, fasc. 1 (January-March), pp. 3-6.

1912 G. PETTINA, *Vicenza*, Bergamo.

1915 B. C. K., "Giovanni Antonio Fasolo," in Thieme-Becker, *Künstlerlexicon*, XXIII.

1924 G. LOUKOMSKI, *Andrea Palladio*, Munich.

1926 G. LOUKOMSKI, "Soffitti monumentali a Vicenza," in *Le Vie d'Italia*, XXXII, I, pp. 61-69.

L. ONGARO, "Cenni storici della Loggia del Capitaniato," in *La Provincia di Vicenza*, 13 and 14 May, nos. 112-113.

1928 G. FIOCCO, *Paolo Veronese*, Bologna.

1929 G. FASOLO, *Le ville del vicentino*, Vicenza.

A. VENTURI, *Storia dell'arte italiana*, Vol. IX, pt. iv, Milan.

1930 G. FASOLO, *Note d'arte*, Vicenza.

1932 A. VENTURI, "Giovanni Antonio Fasolo," in *Enciclopedia Italiana*, XIV.

1941 H. PÉE, *Die Palastbauten des Andrea Palladio*, Würzburg.

1944 R. PALLUCCHINI, *La pittura veneziana del Cinquecento*, Vol. II, Novara.

1945 A. PALLUCCHINI, "La mostra dei cinque secoli di pittura veneta," in *Emporium*, CII, pp. 3-20.

R. PALLUCCHINI, *Cinque secoli di pittura veneta. Catalogo della mostra*, Venice.

1947 E. ARSLAN, "Appunti su Domenico Brusasorci e la sua cerchia," in *Emporium*, CVI, pp. 15-28.

1953 F. BARBIERI, "Loggia Bernarda," in *Guida di Vicenza* (1st ed.), Vicenza, pp. 94-95.

F. BARBIERI (II) "Palazzo di Giustizia," in *Guida di Vicenza* (1st ed.), Vicenza, p. 99.

R. CEVESE, *Le ville vicentine*, Treviso.

L. MAGAGNATO, "Casa Cogollo ora Baroni detta del Palladio," in *Guida di Vicenza* (1st ed.), Vicenza, pp. 158-159.

1956 E. ARSLAN, "Le chiese di Vicenza," in *Cataloghi delle cose d'arte e di antichità d'Italia*, M.P.I., Rome.

F. BARBIERI, "Loggia Bernarda," in *Guida di Vicenza* (2nd ed.), Vicenza, pp. 94-95.

F. BARBIERI (II), "Palazzo di Giustizia," in *Guida di Vicenza* (2nd ed.), Vicenza, p. 99.

L. MAGAGNATO, "Casa Cogollo ora Baroni detta del Palladio," in *Guida di Vicenza* (2nd ed.), Vicenza, pp. 158-159.

1960 G. BARIOLI, "Lavori di riordino e di ripristino in edifici palladiani di proprietà del Comune di Vicenza," in *Bollettino del Centro Internazionale di Studi di Architettura A. Palladio*, II, pp. 133-135.

1961 F. BARBIERI, "Un'opera pressoché ignorata di G. A. Fasolo: le tele per la Loggia del Capitaniato a Vicenza," in *Arte Veneta*, XV, pp. 238-240.

G. M. PILO, *Carpioni*, Venice.

G. G. ZORZI, "Giovanni Antonio Fasolo, pittore lombardo-vicentino, emulo di Paolo Veronese," in *Arte Lombarda*, VI, 2, pp. 209-226.

1962 F. BARBIERI, *Il Museo Civico di Vicenza. Dipinti e sculture dal XVI al XVIII secolo*, Venice.

L. CROSATO, *Gli affreschi nelle ville venete del Cinquecento*, Treviso.

R. PALLUCCHINI, preface to L. Crosato, *Gli affreschi nelle ville venete del Cinquecento*, Treviso, pp. vii-xii.

B. RUPPRECHT, "Gli affreschi cinquecenteschi nelle ville venete," in *Arte Veneta*, XVI, pp. 197-199.

in *Miscellanea in onore di Mario Salmi*, Rome, pp. 331-341.

1963 R. PALLUCCHINI, "Un fregio ignorato di Giulio Carpioni," L. PUPPI, "Giovanni Speranza," in *Rivista dell' Istituto Nazionale d'Archeologia e Storia dell'Arte*, n. s., XI and XII, pp. 370-419.

G. G. ZORZI, "Domenico Groppino di Musso. Un altro architetto lombardo-vicentino imitatore del Palladio," in *Arte Lombarda*, VIII, 2, pp. 114-146.

1964 F. BARBIERI, "Un fregio inedito cinquecentesco nel vicentino palazzo dei Repeta," in *Studi in onore di Antonio Bardella*, Vicenza, pp. 199-206.

G. CANOVA, *Paris Bordone*, Venice.

M. GUIOTTO, "Recenti restauri di edifici palladiani," in *Bollettino del Centro Internazionale di Studi di Architettura A. Palladio*, VI, pt. 2, pp. 70-88.

G. G. ZORZI, *Le opere pubbliche e i palazzi privati di Andrea Palladio*, Venice.

1965 F. LODI, "Un tardo manierista vicentino: Alessandro Maganza," in *Arte Veneta*, XIX, pp. 108-117.

1966 F. DE MAFFEI, "Venetian Perspectivists," *Encyclopedia of World Art*, XI, cols. 229-230.

A. RICCOBONI, "Antonio Zanchi e la pittura veneziana del Seicento," in *Saggi e memorie di Storia dell'Arte*, 5, Florence, pp. 53-135.

M. SALMI, "Late Renaissance Painting," *Encyclopedia of World Art*, XII, cols. 112-121.

1968 F. BARBIERI, *La Basilica Palladiana*, Vicenza.

F. BARBIERI (II), "Il patrimonio artistico della parrocchia," in *La parrocchia di S. Pietro in Vicenza*, Vicenza, pp. 11-70.

R. PALLUCCHINI, "Giambattista Zelotti e Giovanni Antonio Fasolo," in *Bollettino del Centro Internazionale di Studi di Architettura A. Palladio*, X, pp. 203-228.

G. G. ZORZI, *Le ville e i teatri di Andrea Palladio*, Venice.

1970 F. BARBIERI, *The Basilica of Andrea Palladio*, University Park.

INDEX OF PERSONS AND PLACES

Proper names are in capital letters, place names in italics. Numbers in italics indicate the pages in the text with illustrastions.

Abbreviations: a. = architect; st. = stone-carver; m. = mason; p. = painter; s. = sculptor.

ILLUSTRATIONS IN THE TEXT

PLATES

33   Loggia del Capitaniato: detail of the right side of the arch on the façade facing Contra' del Monte, showing the statue of *Victory*

34   Loggia del Capitaniato. LORENZO RUBINI (?): the statue of *Peace* at the left of the arch on the Contra' del Monte side

35   Loggia del Capitaniato. LORENZO RUBINI (?): the statue of *Victory* at the right of the arch on the Contra' del Monte side

36   Loggia del Capitaniato: detail showing the lower part of the façade facing the Piazza

37   Loggia del Capitaniato: detail showing the pedestal on the side facing Contra' del Monte

38   Loggia del Capitaniato: the north side of the portico (interior)

39   Loggia del Capitaniato: the south side of the portico (interior), with the Basilica in the background

40   Loggia del Capitaniato: the east side of the portico (interior)

41   Loggia del Capitaniato: the west side of the portico (interior)

42   Loggia del Capitaniato: the southwest corner of the portico (interior)

43   Loggia del Capitaniato: detail of the southeast corner of the portico (interior)

44   Loggia del Capitaniato: the niche at the back of the portico, with an entrance to the main staircase

45   Loggia del Capitaniato: the central vault of the portico seen from the niche leading to the main staircase

46   Loggia del Capitaniato: view of the back of the portico (interior)

47   Loggia del Capitaniato: view of the back of the portico (interior)

48   Loggia del Capitaniato: door in the niche at the back of the portico, leading to the main staircase

49   Loggia del Capitaniato: door in the north side of the portico

50   Loggia del Capitaniato: the interior of the hall

51   Loggia del Capitaniato: coffered ceiling of the hall. Canvases by Giovanni Antonio Fasolo

52   Loggia del Capitaniato. GIOVANNI ANTONIO FASOLO: *Marcus Curtius Plunging into the Chasm*

53   Loggia del Capitaniato. GIOVANNI ANTONIO FASOLO: *Mutius Scaevola before Porsenna*

54   Loggia del Capitaniato. GIOVANNI ANTONIO FASOLO: *Horatius Cocles Defending the Bridge*

55   Loggia del Capitaniato. GIOVANNI ANTONIO FASOLO: a scene from Roman history

56   Loggia del Capitaniato. GIOVANNI ANTONIO FASOLO: a scene from Roman history

57   Loggia del Capitaniato. GIOVANNI ANTONIO FASOLO: *Titus Manlius Torquatus Killing the Gaul*

58   Loggia del Capitaniato. GIOVANNI ANTONIO FASOLO: a scene from Roman history

COLOR PLATES

a)   Loggia del Capitaniato: general view

b)   Loggia del Capitaniato: façade facing Piazza dei Signori (before 1932)

SCALE DRAWINGS

THE SCALE DRAWINGS WERE EXECUTED BY ANDRZEJ PERESWIET
SOŁTAN UNDER THE DIRECTION OF PROF. MARIO ZOCCONI

PLATES

1 - Vicenza. Loggia del Capitaniato in its setting in Piazza dei Signori,
seen from the Torre di Piazza; the building at right is the Monte di Pietà

2 - Loggia del Capitaniato: façade facing Piazza dei Signori

3 - Loggia del Capitaniato: general view

4 - Loggia del Capitaniato: general view

5 - Loggia del Capitaniato: general view

6 - Loggia del Capitaniato: façade facing Piazza dei Signori (before 1932)

7 - Loggia del Capitaniato: façade facing Piazza dei Signori,
including a portion of the façade on Contra' del Monte

8 - Loggia del Capitaniato: detail of the giant order of the main façade,
with portions of the entablature and ornament of the side façade

9 - Loggia del Capitaniato: detail of the façade facing the Piazza, showing the pseudo-attic

10 - Loggia del Capitaniato: detail showing two bays of the façade facing the Piazza

11 - Loggia del Capitaniato: detail of the left and central bays of the façade facing the Piazza

12 - Loggia del Capitaniato: detail of the central bay of the façade facing the Piazza

13 - Loggia del Capitaniato: detail of the right bay of the façade facing the Piazza,
showing the profile of the side façade

14 - Loggia del Capitaniato: detail of the first storey, oblique view from below

15 - Loggia del Capitaniato: detail of the first storey of the façade facing the Piazza

16 - Loggia del Capitaniato: view of the first storey and the attic of the façade facing the Piazza

17 - Loggia del Capitaniato: view of the corner between Piazza dei Signori and Contra' del Monte

18 - Loggia del Capitaniato: side facing Contra' del Monte, showing the remains of the Torre Verlata

19 - Loggia del Capitaniato: detail of the side facing Contra' del Monte

20 - Loggia del Capitaniato: detail of the lower order of the side facing Contra' del Monte

21 - Loggia del Capitaniato: detail of the lower part of the side facing Contra' del Monte

22 - Loggia del Capitaniato: detail of the first storey, showing the central Serliana and part of the order below

23 · Loggia del Capitaniato: detail of the balcony on the side facing Contra' del Monte, showing the architrave with Palladio's name

24 - Loggia del Capitaniato: detail of the left side of the arch on the façade facing Contra' del Monte

25 - Loggia del Capitaniato: detail of the right side of the arch on the façade facing Contra' del Monte

26 - Loggia del Capitaniato. LORENZO RUBINI: coat-of-arms of the city of Vicenza,
at the left of the arch on the Contra' del Monte side

27 - Loggia del Capitaniato. LORENZO RUBINI: coat-of-arms of the captain Gian Battista Bernardo, at the right of the arch on the Contra' del Monte side

28 - Loggia del Capitaniato: detail of the first storey, showing the decorations by Lorenzo Rubini and the statue of *Virtue* at the left of the Serliana on the Contra' del Monte side

29 - Loggia del Capitaniato: detail of the first storey, showing the decorations by Lorenzo Rubini and the statue of *Honor* at the right of the Serliana on the Contra' del Monte side (the brickwork at the right is part of the Torre Verlata)

30 - Loggia del Capitaniato: detail of the Serliana on the side facing Contra' del Monte,
showing the statue of *Fides*

31 - Loggia del Capitaniato: detail of the Serliana on the side facing Contra' del Monte, showing the statue of *Pietas*

32 - Loggia del Capitaniato: detail of the left side of the arch on the façade facing Contra' del Monte, showing the statue of *Peace*

33 - Loggia del Capitaniato: detail of the right side of the arch on the façade facing Contra' del Monte, showing the statue of *Victory*

34 - Loggia del Capitaniato. LORENZO RUBINI (?):
the statue of *Peace* at the left of the arch on the Contra' del Monte side

35 - Loggia del Capitaniato. Lorenzo Rubini (?):
the statue of *Victory* at the right of the arch on the Contra' del Monte side

36 · Loggia del Capitaniato: detail showing the lower part of the façade facing the Piazza

37 - Loggia del Capitaniato: detail showing the pedestal on the side facing Contra' del Monte

38 - Loggia del Capitaniato: the north side of the portico (interior)

39 - Loggia del Capitaniato: the south side of the portico (interior), with the Basilica in the background

40 - Loggia del Capitaniato: the east side of the portico (interior)

41 - Loggia del Capitaniato: the west side of the portico (interior)

42 - Loggia del Capitaniato: the southwest corner of the portico (interior)

43 - Loggia del Capitaniato: detail of the southeast corner of the portico (interior)

44 - Loggia del Capitaniato: the niche at the back of the portico, with an entrance to the main staircase

45 - Loggia del Capitaniato: the central vault of the portico seen from the niche leading to the main staircase

46 - Loggia del Capitaniato: view of the back of the portico (interior)

47 - Loggia del Capitaniato: view of the back of the portico (interior)

48 - Loggia del Capitaniato: door in the niche at the back of the portico, leading to the main staircase

49 - Loggia del Capitaniato: door in the north side of the portico

50 - Loggia del Capitaniato: the interior of the hall

51 - Loggia del Capitaniato: coffered ceiling of the hall. Canvases by Giovanni Antonio Fasolo

52 - Loggia del Capitaniato. GIOVANNI ANTONIO FASOLO: *Marcus Curtius Plunging into the Chasm*

53 - Loggia del Capitaniato. GIOVANNI ANTONIO FASOLO: *Mutius Scaevola before Porsenna*

54 - Loggia del Capitaniato. GIOVANNI ANTONIO FASOLO: *Horatius Cocles Defending the Bridge*

55 - Loggia del Capitaniato. GIOVANNI ANTONIO FASOLO: a scene from Roman history

56 - Loggia del Capitaniato. GIOVANNI ANTONIO FASOLO: a scene from Roman history

57 - Loggia del Capitaniato. GIOVANNI ANTONIO FASOLO: *Titus Manlius Torquatus Killing the Gaul*

58 - Loggia del Capitaniato: GIOVANNI ANTONIO FASOLO: a scene from Roman history

SURVEY REPORT

THE SURVEY WAS EXECUTED BY ANDRZEJ PERESWIET
SOŁTAN UNDER THE DIRECTION OF PROF. MARIO ZOCCONI

CORSO PALLADIO

CONTRA DEL MONTE

PIAZZA DEI SIGNORI

a - Loggia del Capitaniato: general plan

0   10   50m

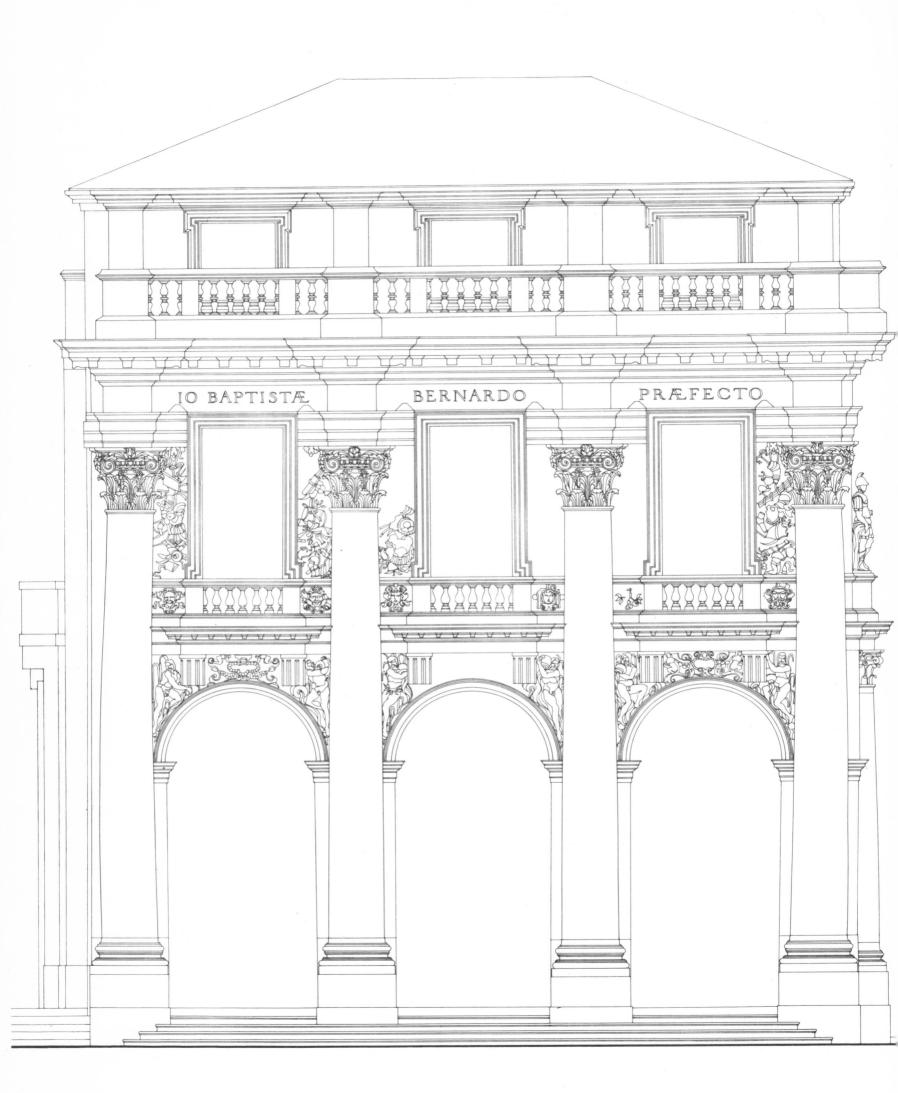

b - Loggia del Capitaniato: façade facing Piazza dei Signori

CIVITA AVIT

ANDREA PALLADIO I ARCHIT.

c - Loggia del Capitaniato: façade facing Contra' del Monte

0   1   5m

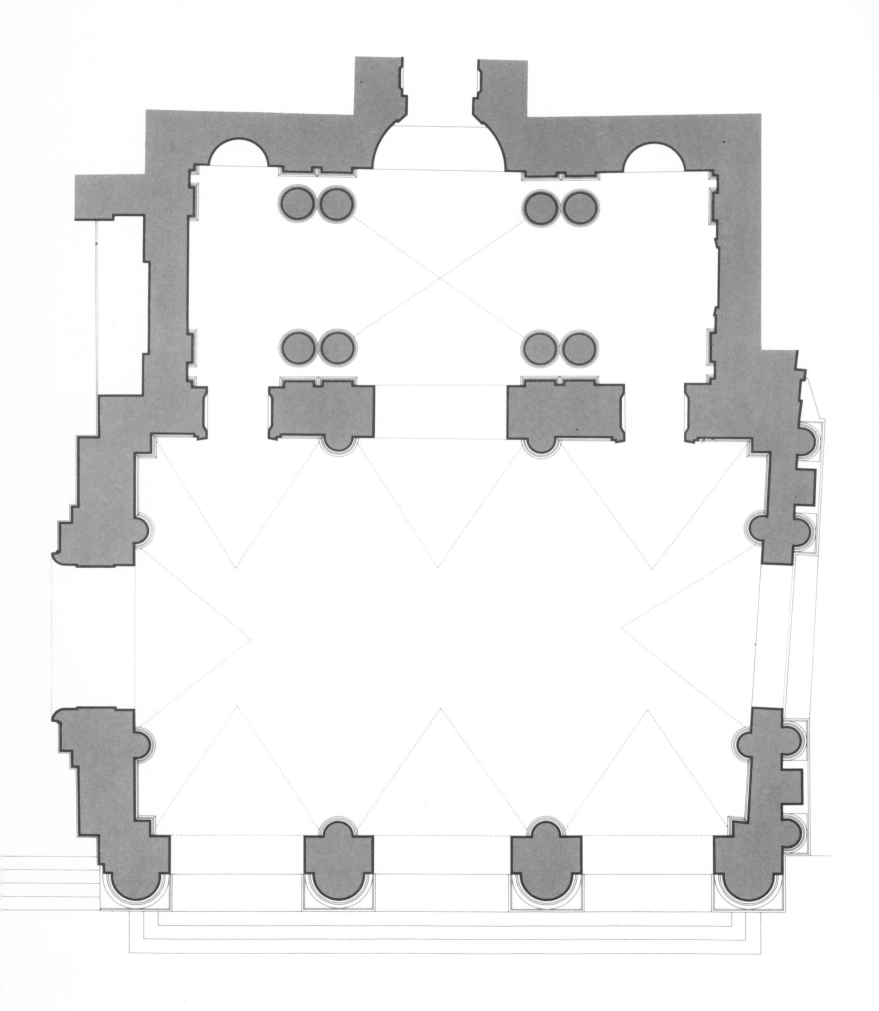

d - **Loggia** del Capitaniato: plan of the ground floor

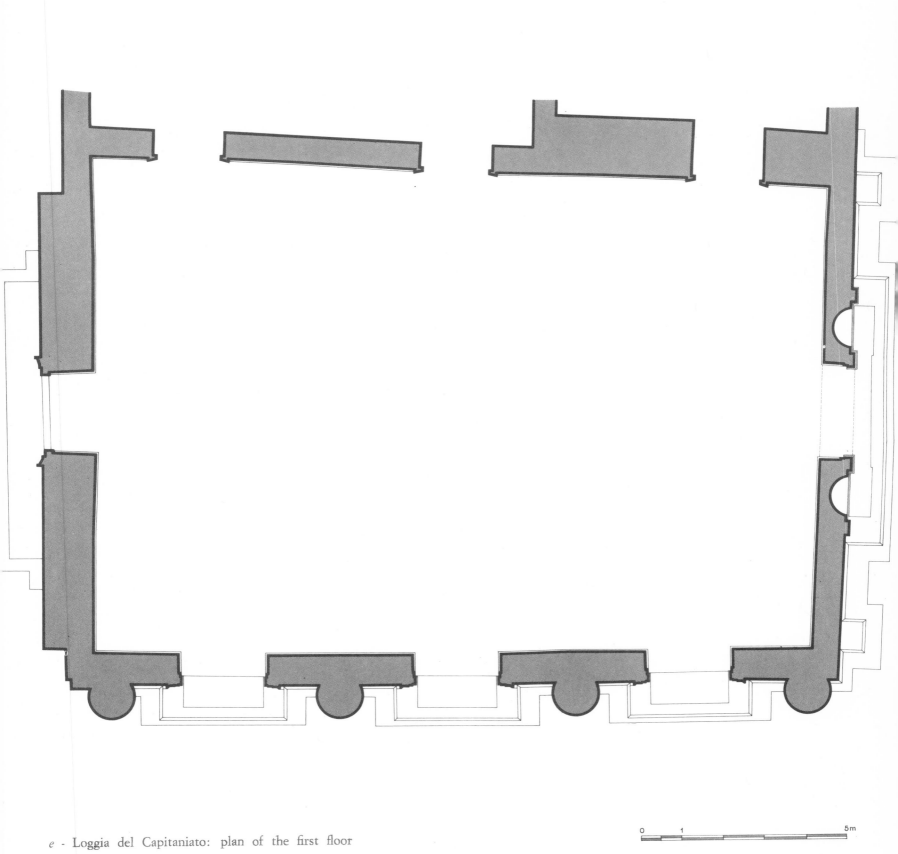

e - Loggia del Capitaniato: plan of the first floor

0   1   5m

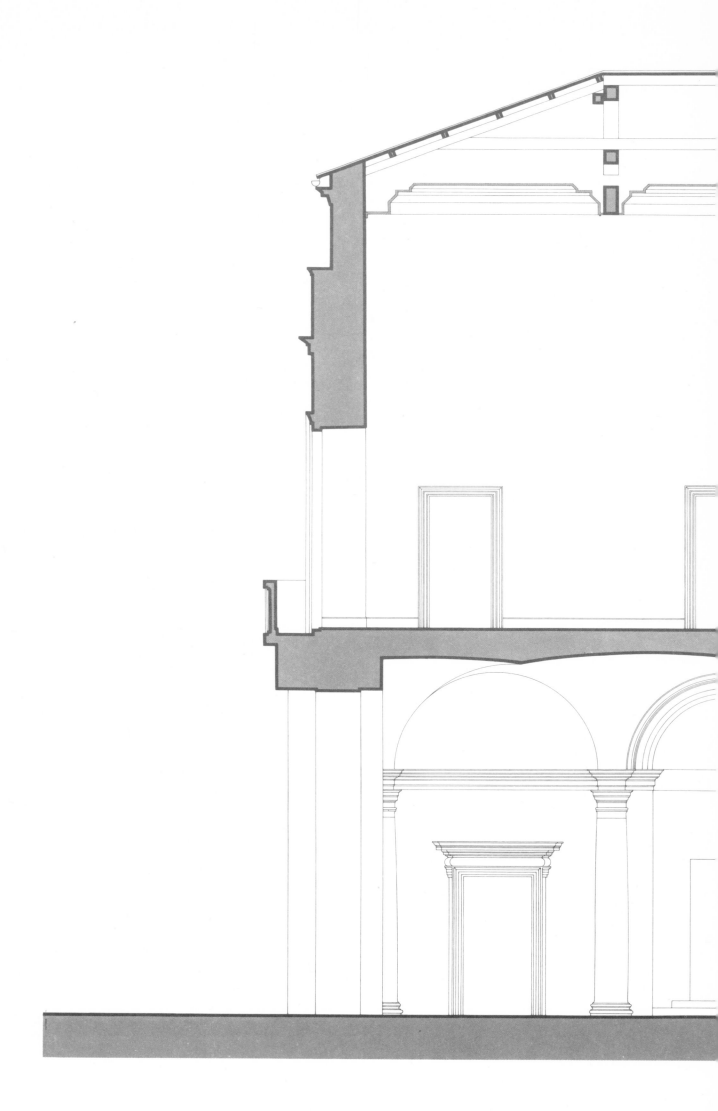

f - Loggia del Capitaniato: longitudinal section

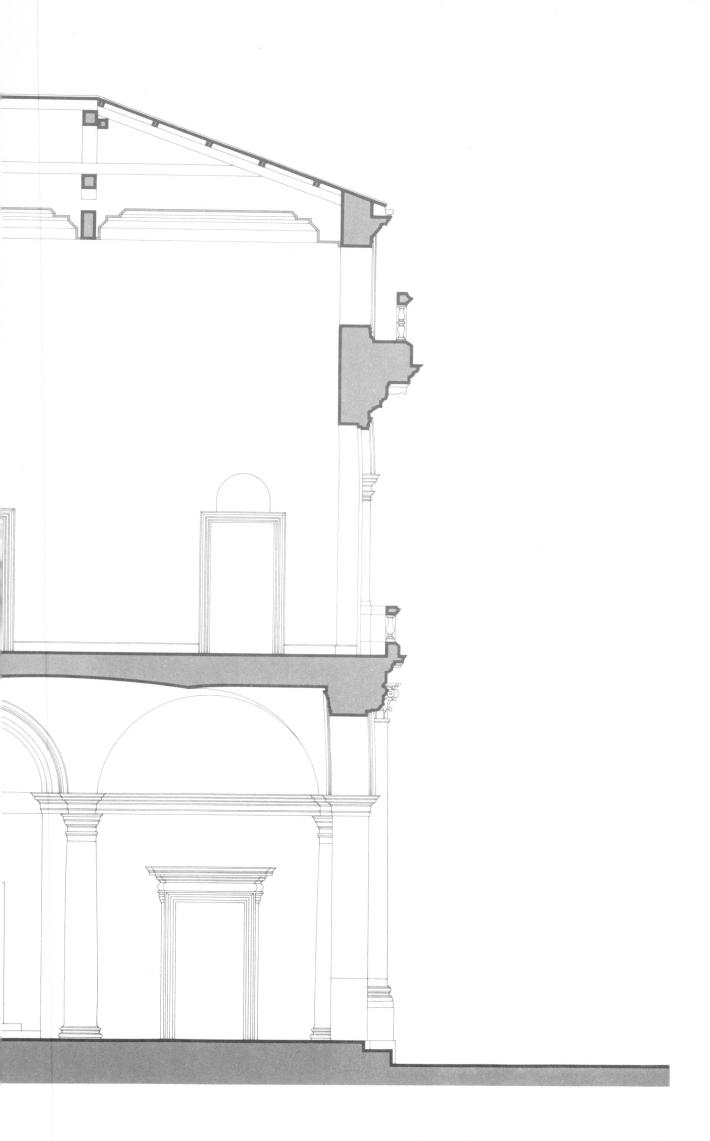

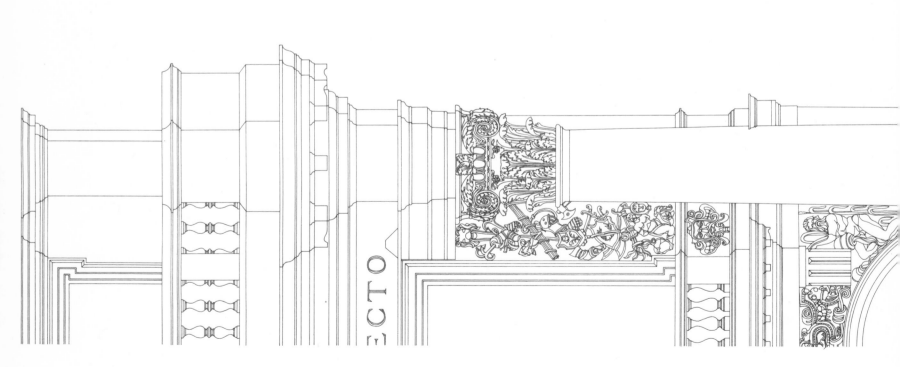

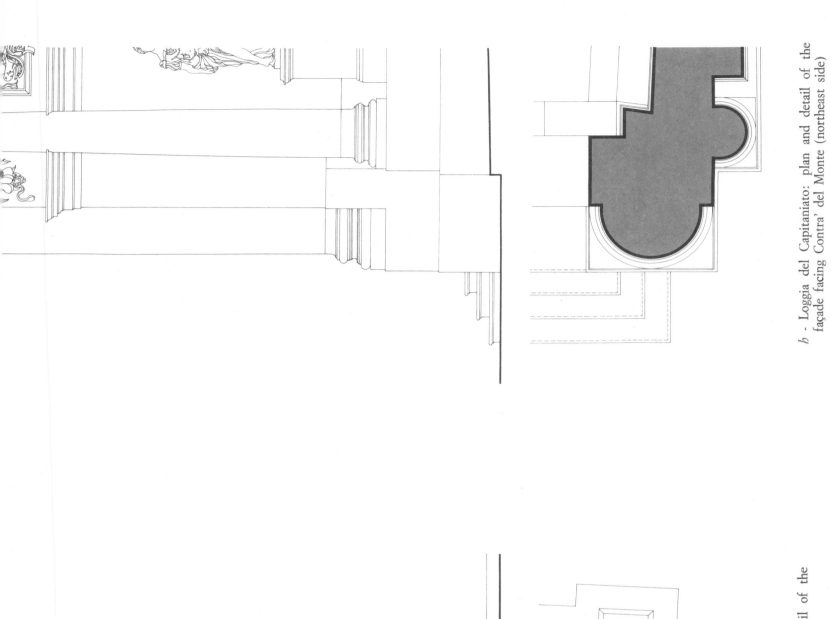

b - Loggia del Capitaniato: plan and detail of the façade facing Contra' del Monte (northeast side)

g - Loggia del Capitaniato: plan and detail of the façace facing Piazza dei Signori

0   1   3m

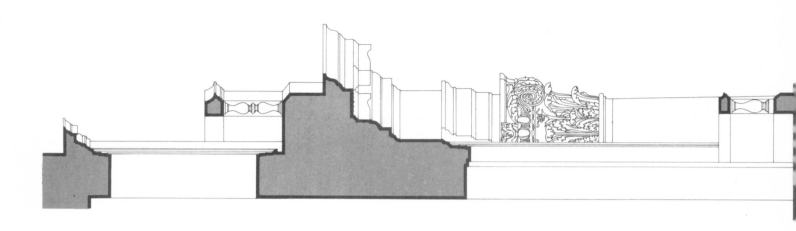

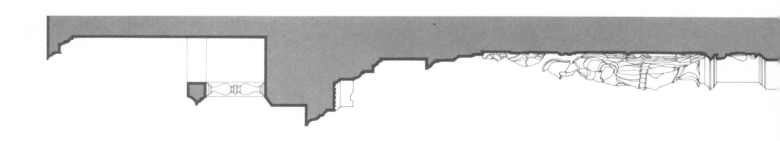

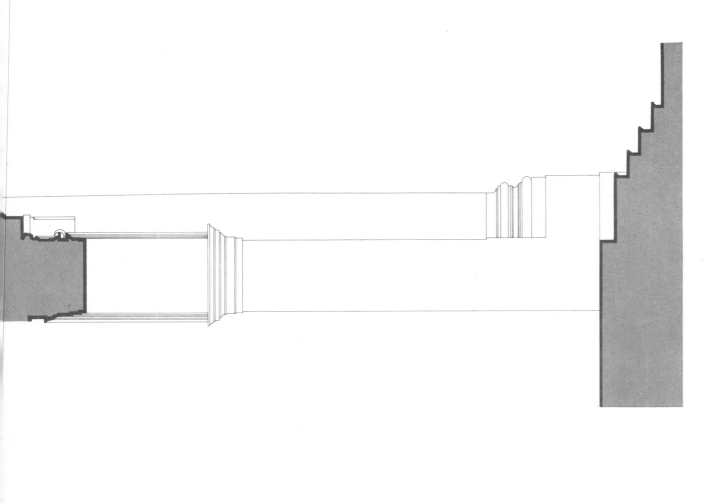

j - Loggia del Capitaniato: detail of a vertical section
of the façade facing Piazza dei Signori

i - Loggia del Capitaniato: detail of a vertical section
of the façade facing Contrà del Monte